Praise for *How Children Become Violent*

"This is a wonderful page-turner about the roots of violence and the power that mental health prevention and early intervention can have on a child's development...It is an undeniably compelling book that every mental health clinician should read...[offering] a fascinating look at the evolution of violence in our society and how it can be prevented."

Deana Krizan, MSW, MPP
Director of Public Policy
Mental Health Association of Maryland

"Kathy Seifert offers a broad and cogent view of the development of aggression and violence in children and adolescents, and richly illustrates the role of interpersonal attachment and social connectedness in the process. Describing the disruption of childhood attachment as a cornerstone in the development of troubled behavior and violence, Dr. Seifert demonstrates the need for lay persons and professionals alike to pay attention to attachment patterns and needs in our child-rearing practices and in our later treatment interventions with troubled children and adolescents. In so doing, she provides us with a perspective and the tools to recognize and assess attitudinal, emotional, and behavioral difficulties that may signal aggression in children and a multi-dimensional approach to treatment that can help in our treatment of these youth and the prevention of further aggression."

Dr. Phil Rich, Ed.D., LICSW
Clinical Director, Stetson School
Barre, Massachusetts

"Dr. Seifert has woven an interesting tapestry of attachment theories, violent behavior problems, and psychopathy literature in making her case regarding disrupted attachment patterns as foundational to violence among youth today. Her use of attachment-based interventions in applied settings encourages early intervention before neurodevelopmental behavioral problems become engrained. Full of information couched in a casual writing style, Dr. Seifert paints the picture of how serious the issues are while also offering many excellent ideas for intervention. I would recommend this book for school personnel, family practitioners, therapists, and social workers."

Gerry D. Blasingame, MA
Licensed Marriage and Family Therapist
New Directions to Hope
Redding, CA

"*How Children Become Violent* is a timely and welcome contribution, addressing one of the most challenging issues of our time: violence, and how to assess, treat, and prevent it in our children and youth. The book is written in an engaging, clear and down-to-earth manner, and will serve as an invaluable resource for all of us — professionals, researchers, parents, and teachers — concerned with the future of our children, families, and communities."

Kenneth I. Maton
Professor of Psychology
University of Maryland, Baltimore County, Psychology Department

How Children Become Violent:
Keeping Your Kids out of Gangs, Terrorist Organizations, and Cults

Kathryn Seifert, Ph.D.

How Children Become Violent:
Keeping Your Kids out of Gangs, Terrorist Organizations, and Cults

Kathryn Seifert, Ph.D.

Boston, Massachusetts
www.AcanthusPublishing.com

Published by Acanthus Publishing
a division of The Ictus Group, LLC
343 Commercial St
Unit 214, Union Wharf
Boston, MA 02109

This book provides information on the history of, causes and effects of, and treatment and therapies for problems affecting the human mind. However, it is not intended to take the place of the professional advice of a psychiatrist or mental health care professional.

In compliance with existing legal and ethical requirements, all identifying details regarding the client(s)/patient(s) discussed in this book, including but not limited to name, age, race, occupation, and place of residence have been altered to prevent recognition.

All information about clinical studies and assessments is the opinion of the author and not an endorsement or guarantee of their efficacy.

Behavioral Objective Sequence abstract reprinted with the permission of Dr. Sheldon Braaten.
The Juvenile Risk Assessment Tool abstract reprinted with the permission of Phil Rich.
Quote from 1966 Philadelphia Public School District 3 presentation reprinted with the permission of Dr. Crowther.
The section in Chapter 11 on Community Mental Health and Treatment was reprinted with the permission of Abigail Malcolm, Psy.D.

Publisher's Cataloging-in-Publication Data
(Prepared by The Donahue Group, Inc.)

Seifert, Kathryn.
How children become violent : keeping your kids out of gangs, terrorist organizations, and cults / Kathryn Seifert.

    p. : ill., charts ; cm.

Includes bibliographical references.
ISBN-10: 1-933631-48-1
ISBN-13: 978-1-933631-48-6

1. Violence in children--Psychological aspects. 2. Violence in children--Prevention. 3. Children and violence--Psychological aspects. 4. Children and violence--Prevention. 5. Attachment disorder in children--Treatment. 6. Child mental health. I. Title.

RJ506.V56 S456 2006
618.92/8582

ISBN-10: 1-933631-48-1
ISBN-13: 978-1-933631-48-6

Cover Design: Domonic Gunn
Interior Layout: Julie Reilly

For my mother and my grandmother,
the kindest, sweetest women I ever knew.

As I take my coffee cup,
The one with roses that I got from you,
I remember with a tear
How I filled that cup for you
Many years ago.

You helped to make me
Who I am.
Look how far I've come.
I hope you're taking a bow
In heaven for what you helped create.

Contents

September 15, 2006

Perhaps it was divine providence that kept me from writing this foreword until a few short hours after a 25-year-old Laval, Quebec resident turned the corridors of Montreal's Dawson College into a bloody target range, killing (as of this writing) one student and wounding 19 others. He then ended his own troubled life with a single shot entering from below his chin.

This vain and otherwise meaningless act follows a string of school-centered violence most notably traced back to Columbine, but, in contradistinction to suggestions in the resulting film documentary by Michael Moore, extreme and irrational aggression is not the sole province of America flowing from its right to bear arms. We in the "Great White North" also known as Canada have our share of children who've fallen through similar cracks. It happens in small towns such as Taber, Alberta, as well as large cosmopolitan cities like Montreal. It was in this same city when in 1989 another 25-year-old, Marc Lepine, killed 14 female engineering students at the Ecole Polytechnique, ending his own life with a single bullet as well.

My good colleague, Dr. Kathryn Seifert, has written a book that many of us would like to write. It addresses a theme that she has felt passionately about throughout her professional life, and she writes about it from her own perspective and on her own terms. Dr. Seifert's efforts throughout her stellar career have been aimed at the noble goal of eliminating the seeds of violence. She focuses on unthinking and unfeeling youth and young adults who commit the senseless destruction we see in Canada, the U.S., and all over the world. A unique characteristic of this book is that is begins with a rigorous yet highly readable account of Attachment Theory of biopsychosocial development, and shows how abuse and neglect of our children leads them to grow up without a modicum of sensitivity to their inner selves or consideration of others. Gathering evidence from both personal experience and archival data, Dr. Seifert demonstrates that this type of violence is neither a North American nor a Western phenomenon—it exists all over the world. She shows the exciting possibility of commonality between Attachment Disorders and the construct of Psychopathy, long recognized as a touchstone of potential violence in adolescents and adults.

Beyond the theoretical, Dr. Seifert goes on to describe a range of compatible (and likely converging) methods for identifying children and youth at elevated risk for developing into violent and hyper-violent young adults. Her own instrument, the CARE (with its Attachment subscale) is unique in its theoretical grounding being coupled with an empirically impressive prediction capability that suggests specific interventions related to unique identified patterns of risk and protective factors.

The professional reader will become better acquainted with an integrated set of theoretically sound, empirically supported, and practically applied tools to practice more effectively as a forensic

mental health professional. The lay reader will find the book somewhat challenging but eminently comprehensible and well worth
the effort. The policy implications would include the necessity for
governments everywhere to invest in education of parenting goals,
responsibilities, and practices as elements of core curricula. Traditional ways of transmitting these values and our most important
interpersonal interactions in a materialistic and fast-moving world
is sadly ineffective as succeedingly larger numbers of youth grow up
detached from parents and positive societal values. There are also
practical and effective instructions for dealing with those who have
already been damaged by their past parenting. This reader-friendly
treatise is particularly appealing for psychology colleagues open to
considering the neurobiological underpinnings of the psychopathy and
aggression constructs.

Dr. Seifert's clinical wisdom shines through the pages of the book as
does her empathy for the victims and concern—but never excuses—for
the perpetrators. This is a very difficult tightrope to walk. It seems
that since Freud claimed to "understand" the causes of pathological
behaviour, mental health professionals have (or at least have been
seen to have) absolved the worst actors of accountability. After all,
if the heinous behaviour was caused by abnormal environments and
their influences, how can we hold the disadvantaged youth responsible? He or she then becomes a victim and society the guilty party.
This lack of personal responsibility removes another potential inhibi-
tory barrier from the personal control armamentarium and likely
contributes incrementally to expression of violence.

In closing, I would like to thank Dr. Seifert for this opportunity to
meaningfully participate in a small way in bringing her book to frui-

tion. The book has provided me with a number of insights that I plan to incorporate into my own research and practice. She is to be congratulated for maintaining her reasoned and principled perspective in bringing forth this integrative and practical treatise that has the potential to help society invest in the long-term good for a modest short-term investment.

Shalom,

David Nussbaum, Ph.D.
Department of Life Sciences/Psychology
University of Toronto, Scarborough
and
Forensic Program
Whitby Mental Health Centre
Whitby, Ontario

Preface

This book was written for professionals working in the mental health, child welfare, juvenile justice/criminal justice, and research fields, as well as students studying these fields and individuals affected by violence. I have tried to make *How Children Become Violent* readable for anyone who is interested in this area or is raising a child with attachment problems.

My goal is to make a case for the fact that juvenile and adult violence begins very early in life, and it is both preventable and treatable. I hope that my research and experience, gained through over 30 years in this profession, will demonstrate that society must intervene early in the lives of children living in violent, neglectful, criminal, and substance-dependent families. Appropriate care, safety, and health for all children is in the world's best interest. This is not to justify dangerous behavior by adults. Both adults and adolescents must take responsibility for their behavior. However, if we have the capacity to assess, prevent, and treat violence and sexual offending and to prevent future offending behaviors, to *not* do so is a crime.

Punishment has never been an adequate answer, for in the United States, it is often puritanical and usually useless in protecting society. That is also not to say that dangerous people should not be kept away from society. But while they are sequestered from the general public, we need to do what we can to ensure that they do not repeat their mistakes. This is what my colleagues and I in the preventative and treatment fields of psychology are trying to advance. Social services, juvenile justice, criminal justice, public policy, mental health and addictions treatment, and forensic hospitals need major reform — reform that is based on research and not revenge. A system that does the same old thing and expects different and better results is itself ill.

Some of our mental health and prison systems are in various states of disrepair and breakdown. Others are moving ahead and making very effective changes. One system can learn from another's mistakes and triumphs. This book provides information about the problems of violence — in its various forms of abuse, neglect, and just plain senseless killing — that takes place in this country. These are problems that are seldom handled well by governmental agencies of child welfare, juvenile justice, education, and mental health. This results in more problems, turning into a cycle of youth violence and sexual offending that will potentially continue for generations. However, with the correct intervention this cycle can be broken, which creates a safer environment for all of society.

Introduction

I am a fairly pleasant, easy-going, and non-violent person. However, I do have my "soap box" issues, over which I can get quite riled: child abuse and neglect, family violence, the lack of free and adequate education for all children, and less than the highest quality mental health services for all children and families regardless of the ability to pay for them.

For as long as I can remember, I've had a drive to know why some people grow up to assault or kill and others do not. As I sat down to write this book, I thought about when and where my experience with violence began, back when I first found myself among psychopaths and killers within The Walls.

It was 1988. I was 42 years old and ready to start a new job at an East Coast adult male prison. As I drove up to the facility for the first time, I was struck by the cold, foreboding appearance of the low, grey buildings with their tiny windows peeking out behind huge razor wire-topped fences. That razor wire was enough to give me the chills. It looked like a ghost town — not a single person stirred outside the buildings. I had no idea what to expect, and I wondered if I was crazy to take this job. I walked into a room in which uniformed officers ushered personnel through a metal detector, inspected bags, and checked IDs for entry.

It was my first day as a psychology associate in a relatively new prison located an hour from where I was raised. I had wanted to move closer to my home and family, so when someone had asked, "Do you want a job in this prison?" I said, somewhat impulsive and naïvely, "Sure, why not? Psychology is the same wherever you practice it, right?" And there, as I entered the first of many clunking metal prison doors, I embarked upon a journey that continues to this day.

I had a small frame and was quite thin at the time, with dark shoulder-length hair and dark round eyes. I have always looked younger than my age — I must have seemed like a babe in the woods surrounded by lots of big, bad, hungry wolves. I'm sure some were thinking, *Boy she won't last long.* But I toughened up fast. You have to if you work within The Walls.

After I walked in for the first time, each door mechanically banged close behind me. I found myself totally enclosed in a very small room of metal and glass. My heart was racing, and I thought to myself, *There's no turning back now.* It's a good thing I don't have claustrophobia — you can't have claustrophobia and work in a jail. A man came in, Dr. Dale Wentworth, who would become my mentor. Dr. Wentworth was an elderly psychiatrist — a character, if you will, who taught me much and had his own way of doing things. Even though we worked in a prison with a myriad of dangerous inmates, it was before we had the ability to judge who was truly at risk for being violent in the future and who was not. I would pay dearly for this lack of knowledge by placing myself both unnecessarily and unwittingly in some very dangerous situations.

"Make a habit of writing down your thoughts and experiences every day," Dr. Wentworth said to me. "You may want to write about this in the future."

Unfortunately, I didn't follow Dr. Wentworth's advice. The pace for a psychologist in a large prison is hectic and stressful. If I found a minute to sit, I was trying to shake off the sights and sounds and events of the week — it could have been anything from a cut up, bleeding inmate, to one running naked through the school — or one who had not come out of his cell for ten years. Then there was the one who repeatedly threatened to kill himself, or the one who claimed I took off his leg every night and used it for a golf club. As you can see, there was always plenty to do, and plenty on my mind. Even though I didn't write my experiences down then, the memories are still so vivid that I wouldn't even need notes in front of me. So here I am, Dr. Wentworth, writing this book, and composing my experiences mostly from memory.

There were many events that shaped my way of thinking while working both at this prison and in several other criminal justice facilities. I hope those who were there will forgive any lapses in memory, and also remember that I have changed names, settings, and circumstances to protect both the innocent and the not-so-innocent.

Working in a prison meant learning to adapt to a completely new environment. In this prison, inmates lived in housing units and each unit had several different locked and separate wings. In the center was a glass and metal enclosure for officers to run electronic doors, as well as watch and manage all activities. There was a separate chow, chapel, gym, medical and mental health unit, and school. In the center were "yards," or large open spaces, with walkways for inmates to pass from one location to another. The cells were just like what you've seen on TV: small, with a bed, a toilet, and a sink. Most cells were inhabited by two men. I had to ignore hoots, cat calls, and obscenities constantly shouted at me from the small slit exterior windows cut into the drab, gray concrete walls of the segregation unit. The voices could be high-pitched and creepy; they made you want to go home and wash. My stomach turned into knots in this atmosphere, but I had to learn to shut the inmate's voices off as if they didn't exist. If I hadn't, then it would have made working there unbearable — maybe I would have even gone crazy.

While it could be very dangerous behind The Walls, most days were uneventful. Camaraderie existed among the correctional employees because we knew at any moment we might find ourselves depending on a coworker for our safety — or maybe even our lives. This closeness gave us a sense of protection so that we could go about our daily routine. You cannot constantly feel afraid or unsafe and do your job *and* remain sane. It's like having an "on-guard" sense of being mostly safe but not completely, so you always watch for any signs that a situation could become unsafe. Unsafe situations can happen in an instant when you work in a prison, and everybody who works there knows it.

It was within The Walls that I met several very dangerous psychopaths. I also observed among this population every psychiatric disorder that I had ever read about in my abnormal psychology books, but might not otherwise have seen in person. There was catalepsy, or, more descriptively, "waxy flexibility" (allowing one's posture to be rearranged, holding the new position for long periods of time) and hysterical conversion reaction (a belief that a limb is paralyzed when it is not). It was a great training experience because I was able to study and treat many obscure behaviors. One man kept telling us, "My time is up, my time is up." Over and over again, he repeated, "My time is up." No one paid attention or knew what he meant until it was discovered that his time actually was up — he had served his full sentence and was released. One man cut himself and mixed his blood with water and splashed it all over his cell. One man wrote "and twenty five" over and over again, day in and day out for years. Then there was the inmate who could and would swallow anything from a TV antenna to glass to a ballpoint pen because it got him a ride out of the prison hospital to the community hospital.

A few faces and events have remained etched vibrantly in my memory, and I can recall scenarios as if they happened yesterday. I remember walking down a tier in a flax jacket (a Kevlar vest that protects your chest from being injured if someone should try to stab you). I was attempting to coax a mentally ill inmate who was bleed- ing to death to come peacefully out of his barricaded cell so he would not have to be taken out by force. He would not listen to me and was taken out of the cell by correctional officers and brought to the hospital.

Normally the cell blocks smelled of bleach and floor wax. It was actually quite antiseptic and orderly until the days when the inmates got into uproars and threw urine, feces, or burning paper into the corridors. Then the hallways would smell foul, and a horrible stench would permeate the walls. I don't know why they'd throw these things at us — be it of anger, revenge, or just for kicks. Who knows what's going on in the mind of a mentally ill person who's locked up for 23 hours a day? The mix of body odor, the smell of urine and feces, and the reek of burning paper is a smell you can never quite forget.

Numerous staff members have been raped, injured, or killed while working in the criminal justice system trying to offer these psychopaths a second chance at life. This fact is also something you never totally shake off. Luck and fate were the sole determinants as to who was assaulted: them or you.

Officers were often called in to protect my colleagues and I to prevent dangerous incidents, and sometimes to save our lives. One learns quickly that you need to always be aware and careful in a prison, and correctional officers are your lifelines if you choose to work behind The Walls.

On one particular day I was talking to a group of inmates in the day room. Officers were used to seeing me talking to groups of inmates; I did it all the time. But this time I hadn't noticed a fight brewing in the far corner. I let my guard down for an instant and there I was, trapped in the day room in the midst of a full-fledged brawl. Anyone in my line of work knows that if you get caught in the day room when a fight breaks out, you are on your own until substantial help arrives. You don't open the day room doors after a fight has started until there is sufficient staff to safely assuage the situation. The Tact Team advanced on the other side of the door, making an unmistakable noise that sounded like 1,000 men marching with heavy boots on. As my heart was racing and I truly began to feel that I would be hurt, some of the inmates formed a line between the fight and me, giving me time to get "buzzed" out the door. Buzzed is the word used to describe the sound that's made when an officer presses the release to open an electronic door. *Bzzzzzzzzz!* The door swung open. There was never a sweeter sound in my life. To this day, just thinking about it makes me tense.

Paradoxically, some inmates were completely docile and compliant with the prison rules — some were even polite and helpful. They held responsible jobs in the school or dining hall. Although they had done horrible things before their incarceration, after years of imprisonment it was clear that some inmates weren't very dangerous at all, at least while they had the structure of the prison on which to rely. For many of these guys the internal structure that guides most of us to follow rules simply was not there. These are the ones who haven't had early experiences that engendered trust in others, a positive self-image, feelings of safety and self-efficacy, or a need to follow rules if left to their own devices. They need the external structure of a prison to do well. Without it, they function poorly. I've seen inmates released and returned to jail within 48 hours because they are unable to comply with non-prison rules. That's why the training for new employees emphasizes this important idea: *Never forget who you are dealing with. Politeness and helpfulness can be just a front to suck you in so they can take advantage of you. Never forget where you are.*

One of the greatest predictors of reduced risk for recidivism for all inmates and psychopaths is age. Once past the age of 45 or 50, a prisoner's chance of re-offending is reduced, especially if they have gained a high school education while incarcerated. I remember one inmate that personified this theory; he was a tall man, very polite and docile. He had a job in the dining hall for years. Though he was incarcerated for first-degree murder, when you talked to him, you couldn't imagine why he was in jail. He had grown up serving a prison sentence, and matured from a violent offender into an adult who was compliant with society's rules. He had children that accepted him back home, and he was able to transition back into society as a functioning member. It is likely that his children grew up to be pro-social because he had been locked up most of their lives.

When I look back upon all the sticky situations in which I found myself and every time my life was in jeopardy, I ask myself, *What was I thinking? Day in and day out in the company of psychopaths?* The invincibility that is usually reserved for people in their 20s lasted well into my 40s. I never gave up — granted, I wasn't stabbed or raped like some other prison employees were, but on multiple occasions I found myself in scenarios that could have easily left me with similar or worse injuries. In hindsight, it is these lessons that have helped me to understand crime and violence firsthand.

Over these last three decades as a criminal justice and psychotherapy professional, I have seen countless patients with either severe mental illnesses or histories of grotesquely violent behavior. As I asked them questions and delved into their pasts, it became clear that many, if not all, had experienced some level of childhood trauma in the form of neglectful, painful, or violent upbringings. I then began to ask myself, *Could there be some link between childhood trauma and the inability to lead normal, productive lives and have empathy for others?* I continued to explore this hypothesis, and I have performed years of research with this idea as a paradigm.

After giving hundreds of psychological evaluations, I developed a list of common characteristics that seemed to apply to the majority of the criminal and juvenile justice populations. Early abuse, neglect, and exposure to domestic violence were prominent factors for most of those I tested with criminal or violent backgrounds. I started collecting data that demonstrated the majority of violent and sexual offenders — adult or juvenile, male or female — all had histories of childhood abuse, neglect, traumatic loss of parents without sufficient substitute caregivers, or exposure to domestic violence. I found that the reason my patients could not conform to the rules of society was because of unaddressed traumatic childhoods, or what I call Attachment Problems.

Attachment is the deep and enduring connection established between a child and a caregiver in the first several years of life. Attachments are secure when children are well cared for emotionally and physically, and when the caregiver is consistent and nurturing within appropriate boundaries. Cooing, nursing, talking baby talk, caressing, rocking, socializing, having diapers changed, and being shown unconditional love comprise healthy interactions in which children learn to bond with their caregivers. As it takes place during early years, it is through this bonding that children learn how to participate in relationships with others. Even though they may seem too young and naïve to understand, those little brains are absorbent sponges soaking up everything around them.

Problems with attachment arise when the child's needs are not met — when she soils her diaper and isn't changed, when she's hungry and isn't fed, or when she's neglected in other ways. Attachment is further disrupted when the child lives in a constant atmosphere of domestic violence: of physical, emotional, and/or sexual abuse. In his 1944 study, psychologist John Bowlby hypothesized that disruptions in the attachment experiences of infants result in antisocial and aggressive behaviors later in childhood or adolescence (1998). These disruptions can affect some or all aspects of a child's development. Children with Attachment Disorders, or Disrupted Attachment Patterns (DAP), may lack a conscience and empathy for others. They may torture animals or be the school bully. In my experience, I have found that when children are prevented from attaching to family members and caregivers in early years, they go on to have uncontrollable rages — rages that, if untreated, result in a lifetime of disregulated emotions and behavior, often diagnosed as a personality disorder, and sometimes perpetual violence.

In the Children with Attachment Disorders study I performed s in 2001, 93 percent had chronic and severe behavior problems that began before the age of 13. The same percentage of children were impulsive and had social skill deficits. All had experienced abuse, neglect, or exposure to domestic violence before the age of 4. Furthermore, youth with attachment problems showed a failure to have the necessary neural structures to cope effectively with stress, perform complex cognitive tasks, or establish loving relationships (Perry and Pollard 1997; Hare 1993; Seifert 2003). Nurturing and good caregiving is necessary for normal brain development throughout childhood. The lack of full brain development seen in many violent people is almost always a direct result of head injuries sustained during abuse, brain underdevelopment due to severe infant neglect and malnutrition, and/or failure of neural structure necessary for interpersonal skills to develop due to lack of appropriate nurturing during infancy and early childhood.

All over the world — from Eastern to Western cultures, in upper,

healthy or destructive upbringing
INTRODUCTION XIX
secure or disrupted attachment

middle, and working classes, across racial and ethnic boundaries — children are abused. In the United States alone, there were 3 million cases of child maltreatment reported in 2004; 63 percent were substantiated. In 2004, 1,490 cases of child abuse or neglect ended in the child's death. At the time this book goes to print, four children will die each day at the hands of their parents and caregivers (Gaudiosi, 2004). These statistics rise consistently from year to year. The children who survive carry their traumatic upbringing along with them for the rest of their lives. Some will seek acceptance by joining gangs or harmful religious cults; in extreme cases, some will find refuge in terrorist organizations. Attachment disorders are bound to manifest in destructive ways unless we as a society take the necessary steps to improve our children's living conditions, stop the cycle of violence from continuing, and offer treatment to the abused.

In Part I of this book, I describe the different characteristics of healthy and destructive upbringings and how each facilitates secure and disrupted attachments. I examine the upbringings of several American serial killers, and then look at the dire, poverty-stricken conditions that fuel terrorist organizations abroad. It is striking that no matter where you look, there is a child forgotten or mistreated. It could be the neighborhood reclusive teenager drawn to his uncle's gun collection or an abandoned street kid left to fend for himself. After this general overview of violent tendencies, in Part II I provide methods for identifying risk of violence. I describe several assessment tools and methods useful for therapists, officials, and caretakers. After all, violence is preventable if we know which signs and precursors to target.

Finally, in Part III, I offer treatment procedures for children with DAP and youth at risk for violence. We as a society must take collective responsibility for the welfare of our children, and many of the treatments now available can help us in doing just that. My colleague, Rob Schmidt, LCPC, NCC, offers a final chapter on School-Based Mental Health programs, which illustrate just one part of a multifaceted, complex solution. While School-Based Mental Health programs are just one initiative aiming to treat juvenile mental health problems and combat violence through the schools, they prove that when people pool their resources, efforts, and their hopes for future, we can save our children.

Part 1

Violence and Disrupted Attachment Patterns (DAP)

Chapter 1

Secure and Disrupted Attachments

My maternal grandmother died when my mother was 2 years old. My grandfather felt he couldn't properly raise a little girl on his own, so my aunt and uncle stepped in as her caretakers. At the time, my great aunt and uncle were middle-aged and lived in a small, two-bedroom cottage on Maryland's rural eastern shore. Their house's Victorian style furniture seemed to transport it back in time.

My great aunt, though very warm, was also very proper. She fit in with the house perfectly — never without her Victorian cameos and long crystal-beaded necklaces. Visiting as a little girl, I remember reprimands like, "I am not your 'aunt' [pronounced ant], I am your aunt [pronounced awnt]. Ants are those little black things that crawl on the ground!"

My great aunt and uncle expected good behavior — anything less was unacceptable. I can imagine my mother lying in that peaceful house in her four-poster pineapple wood bed (as I later did growing up in the same house) and listening to the *tick-tock* of the old grandfather clock until she fell asleep at night. My aunt and uncle never raised their voices or argued. They weren't highly demonstrative with physical affection either, but my mom knew she was loved, safe, and would be well taken care of.

Like my mother, my sisters and I were able to form secure attachments as children. I was the eldest of five sisters in a loving and caring family with a mom and dad, grandparents, and other adults who lavished us with love and provided structure and safety to our daily lives. It was a sheltered, carefree childhood full of wonderful memories.

I remember when my sister, Cindy, and I were given our first pair of old-fashioned, strap-on roller skates. Made of metal, with a toe portion adjustable by skate key, Cindy and I learned to use these roller skates by holding onto Daddy's arms as he walked us up and down Locust Street. Can you imagine how comical that was to see a 6 foot 3 man with a little girl on roller skates flanking each side, arms and legs flying in all directions? Needless to say, we knew we were loved.

My best friend before I started school was Judy Richardson, who lived with her family on a large farm. I can remember spending the night and being surrounded and supported by the close family, saying morning prayers with everyone in the long, comfortable living room. Their big yellow tabby cat would curl up next to the huge, deep-green jade plant, sunning herself on the window seat. The lights were dim and there was the fragrant smell of smoke from the ancient wood burning stove and the wonderful smell of eggs, bacon, and biscuits from the kitchen. When I went to the bed that was taller than I was, I needed a step stool to climb into it. It was like *The Waltons* — "Good night,

Judy." "Good night, Jane." "Good night, Kathy." "Good night, Cindy."
"Good night, mom and daddy." "Good night, Mr. and Mrs. Richardson." "Good night, Mother." "Good night, Jim." We felt so safe and
cared for.

Secure Attachment

My mother, my four sisters, the Richardson children, and I were
raised in secure attachment environments. We were clothed, fed,
and schooled and were oblivious to abuse, neglect, and domestic violence. If we experienced any sort of trauma, then someone stepped
in to help us heal. We grew up to raise families and all of us are now
pro-social adults without tendencies toward violence. We learned
how to love, relate positively, have pro-social goals, and raise children the way our parents/caregivers raised us. In fact, most children
will grow up in families that are relatively healthy and in which
parents take good care of their children. These healthy families allow
societies to flourish.

The job of the caregiver is to teach, nurture, care for, and protect
the child. Bonding experiences that positively affect the relationship
between a child and a caregiver also influence the development of
the child biologically, socially, morally, and cognitively. Through the
centuries, the survival of society has depended on our ability to take
care of and protect both our own and our neighbor's families — especially the most vulnerable among us, our children. While Darwin
said it is *survival of the fittest* that ensures the continued existence
of a species, I would refine that further by saying it is also *survival of
the group that cares for its young.* Man would not have survived in
prehistoric times or on the early frontiers if this were not so. Parents

protecting offspring from predators — and the offspring's own mis-chief — has allowed for the next generation to survive and pass on family genes.

While attachments are secure when a child is well cared for, in order for the child to grow and be a productive member of a com-munity, appropriate boundaries must also be set. Most parents don't allow their children to eat candy instead of vegetables, but if a child dislikes spinach, then they may offer carrots as an alterna-tive. They probably won't allow 10-year-olds to drive cars and stay out until midnight. We voted as a country not to allow our youth to drink alcohol, smoke cigarettes, or use drugs. All children must learn the rules of society in order to be good citizens.

Discipline for breaking these rules, however, must be appropriate for the developmental level of the child. Discipline that is too harsh or too weak, absent, or inconsistent is associated with more behavior problems. It is nurturing that fosters attachment, moral develop-ment, and the desire to please adults — and thus a tendency to follow the rules that parents have established. Spanking, a punish-ment with which I disagree, is for the relief of a parent's anger, and is not effective. Discipline must be based upon teaching the child about why the social rule is important and helping him grow devel-opmentally. A lesson must be taught and learned. I recommend a time-out (one minute per year of child's age) or the revoking of a privilege, two means that can be used to encourage the child to think about what he has done. Both should be followed by an explanation of the social rule and how the behavior may have hurt others. In this manner children are taught to see things from another person's point of view (a stage of moral development) — to have *empathy*.

If you've ever watched new mothers hold their infants, they instinctively rock and soothe them. They kiss their babies' foreheads, smile
and coo and speak to them in baby talk. This behavior represents the
most biological and instinctive interactions of humankind. It encourages the child to develop a positive and healthy image of himself,
other people, and relationships (Levy and Orlans 1998). When the
caregiver meets the child's needs, the child learns that the world is
predictable and reasonable. This forms the basis for problem-solving and the ability to relate to and trust others. A child that is loved,
protected, and cared for knows he can trust adults and learn from
them. He benefits from adult interpretations of daily occurrences,
from something as simple as *why it rains on the day I want to go to
the park* to *why my parents are always in charge* and what it means
to have a routine. Everything is learned in this manner.

Thus a child learns that when she is upset, if she cries, a caring and
attentive parent will hug and rock her until she feels better. This
interaction teaches her how to calm herself when she is upset — a
very important developmental skill called self-soothing and self-love.
It means the child is learning to have a positive view of the world
and a positive image of herself as well. This skill will be necessary for
all cooperative social interactions for the rest of her life — and it all
starts as a babe cradled in mama's arms.

In this first year of life, the infant's brain is developing rapidly. Cere-
bral structures and connections are overproduced. Like a bodybuilder
lifting weights to build muscle, the stimulated parts of the child's
brain are those that will strengthen most. Perhaps of equivalent
importance is that those areas that remain unused become dysfunctional and disappear. When a caregiver uses soothing techniques to

calm a child, the amygdyla, a part of the brain that controls affect regulation (our ability to calm ourselves when we are upset), continues to develop. Hearing language strengthens the parts of the brain where language and communication are developed. Reciprocal smiling and games stimulate the parts of the brain that deal with human relationships and emotion.

It is the attachment to the caregiver and fear of loss of the relationship that allows a child to learn the "rules" of society and the culture in which he lives. Setting limits and boundaries is essential to child-rearing. This not only provides the stability and consistency that children rely on for reassurance, it also provides a small underpinning of fear of losing essential relationships if rules are broken. This will maintain motivation for adherence to rules. It is this unconscious, harmless anxiety that encourages the child to sublimate his desires, delay gratification, and focus attention on longer-term goals and values — all essential skills to adult functioning. He learns to behave in the way he believes is pleasing to the adults in his life, thus securing the necessary attachments.

A child will also learn to mimic what he sees adults doing. Children internalize the structure of their society, culture, and family through observation and mimicking what they see. Girls and boys may play house and dress-up or cops and robbers. If the models they see are positive and healthy, then this is what the child will strive to replicate. Children who have healthy attachment experiences with caregivers develop a positive, internal working model of themselves, others, and the world around them. Likewise, if the attachments are unhealthy and destructive, then the child will still try to replicate the pattern, believing violence, abuse, and neglect is what is proper, right, and normal.

And finally, positive caregiver/child bonding experiences protect the youth from developing dangerous, unempathetic personalities and predatorial behavior. Now let's examine some traits and conditions of disrupted attachments.

Figure 1. Internal Working Model for Adaptive Relationships (Adapted from Levy and Orlans, First Year Cycle of Life)

Figure 1. Pre-Verbal Internal Working Model

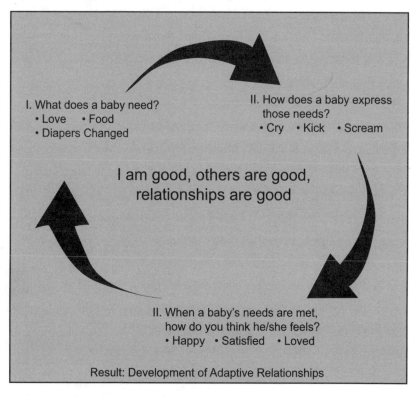

I. What does a baby need?
• Love   • Food
• Diapers Changed

II. How does a baby express those needs?
• Cry   • Kick   • Scream

I am good, others are good, relationships are good

II. When a baby's needs are met, how do you think he/she feels?
• Happy   • Satisfied   • Loved

Result: Development of Adaptive Relationships

Disrupted Attachment: Case Story

James, a baby with curly tendrils of silken black hair, had a mother named Theresa. Theresa's husband beat her savagely on a regular basis and then eventually left. The beatings made Theresa depressed. To deal with her depression, she began to drink. In a constant state of inebriation, Theresa was either unable to hear or simply neglected James when he cried. She would methodically prop his bottle up to feed him, and only change his diaper once a day. James was left in his crib to entertain himself. Sometimes he shivered because he was wet and didn't have any covers to keep him warm. He cried a lot and longed for companionship.

Theresa would spank James when he cried or leave the house altogether to avoid his shrieks. Going to the bar was much more appealing than dealing with dirty diapers and constant tears. It got to the point where Theresa just couldn't stand it any longer. *My life is such a mess*, she thought. *I need adult companionship*. James was more responsibility than she could handle.

James eventually stopped crying because no one, least of all Mom, ever came when he cried. He was hungry and dirty and his diaper rash hurt, but there was nothing he could do.

As James became an adolescent, he found companionship in the only place he could: on the streets. James stole to get what he wanted. He learned at a young age that no one else was going to help, so he had to help himself. He didn't do well in school, skipping class most days. He later joined a gang whose rite of initiation required that he rob a local convenience store.

So, without reservations, James stuffed a .44 Magnum in the waist-band of his jeans and set out for the convenience store. He entered and waved the gun in the owner's face. But before James realized what he was doing, the owner pulled his own gun from behind the counter and planted a bullet in James's forehead. When it was all over, the store owner was shaken up and James lay dead on the floor, his head of unruly black hair outlined by a pool of blood.

This is a sad and disheartening story — a story I have seen repeated over and over again. The characters' names and faces change, yet the destruction and waste of life is always the same. This story illus-trates what happens when attachments are disrupted. It often starts at the hands of an antisocial, attachment disordered, addicted, or mentally ill parent. Theresa was abused by her husband, was an alco-holic, and neglected James. She was unable to appropriately nurture her child or give him adequate amounts of emotional and physical care.

Disrupted Attachment

When a parent or guardian is abusive, neglectful, violent, or unavail-able, the child's ability to attach to the caregiver is reduced, and therefore the internal model of self and others may be negative and disturbed. The resulting attachment disorder or problem is the basis for various dangerous conduct, personality disorders, and adult dysfunctions (Ziegler 1998), including psychopathy (Meloy 2002).

Psychopathy, as defined by Hare (1993), applies to the chronically violent, detached adult who is without conscience or empathy for others. He/she generally commits heinous crimes. These are the people that we hear about on the news who have committed unimaginable crimes, often serial murders, and appear to care nothing about the welfare of others. Some infamous examples etched in all of our memories are Jeffrey Dahmer, Ted Bundy, Son of Sam, the Boston Strangler, and John Wayne Gacy (there is more on serial killers in Chapter 3).

Dr. Frank Gardner studied violent offenders and found that early aversive history was a significant predictor (23 percent of the variance) of adult trait anger. Those with higher levels of trait and reactive anger also had early adverse histories and violent offending. He proposes that there may be two types of violent offending that may require different types of treatment (2006 APA Conference poster presentation). These may be similar to the "hot" (angry, failure to modulate emotion) and "cold" (instrumental, psychopathic, *I want what I want and I want it now!*) violence described in the domestic violence literature.

Many are now examining the connection between childhood trauma and later severe behavioral problems (Forth, et. al. 2003; Seifert 2003; Augimeri, et. al. 1998). Looking at the developmental trajectory may help scientists determine at which point an attachment problem becomes a personality disorder or when youth with trauma take a more normal developmental track. Statistics indicate that 800,000 children with severe attachment disorders are coming to the attention of the child welfare system each year (Levy and Orlans 1998). How many will become violent criminals? How can we stop the progression?

In many attachment disorder cases, emotional, moral, spiritual, cognitive, relationship, and physical development are often significantly injured or delayed. Without attachment, the child does not internalize cultural structure such as laws, traditions, and social norms — or the desire to follow them. Survival means relying on oneself, not others. Thus the child is likely to withdraw into a world of fantasy, fear, and misinterpretation. Later, when other adults such as teachers or therapists may be more available to him, the child may not trust them enough to actually be able to learn from them (Levy and Orlans 1998).

Mistreated children often have more symptoms of Post Traumatic Stress Disorder (PTSD) or complex PTSD (van der Kolk, Silberg, and Waters 2003) such as anxiety, depression, avoidance of events that remind them of their trauma, and exaggerated startle reflex than children who come from more nurturing backgrounds (Perry 1994). They may have nightmares and are prone to dissociate. Their thinking and perceiving are disturbed and inaccurate. Additionally, they over-attribute the hostile intent of others. If someone is abused over and over again throughout childhood, then she would begin to expect to be mistreated. Eventually, she would interpret almost everything as hostile or dangerous, even if it isn't, and react as if everything and everyone poses a threat to her.

Sexually abused children may have odd thinking or speech patterns or reactions. They often have visual and auditory flashbacks that they have difficulty distinguishing from reality. Some have dissociative reactions. They often have closed off their feelings in order to endure the abuse, and so they appear to have no feelings at all. Their responses on the Rorschach (commonly known as the ink blot test) often look more like psychotic responses than they do those of normal children (Gacono and Meloy 1994). Greater proportions of maltreated children have problems with addictions, oppositionality, and conduct disorders than non-mistreated children (Ziegler 1998). In adulthood, these problems develop into various personality disorders such as Narcissistic, Antisocial, Borderline, and Histrionic Personality Disorders.

Abused and severely neglected children seem to be "stuck" in the earlier, more egocentric stages of moral development. At these stages, good behavior is rewarded and bad behavior is punished; adults control the behavior of children rather than the child relying on self-control. Children with DAP have not reached the more mature stages of moral and social development, and neither understand nor spontaneously exhibit the ability to independently monitor and correct their behavior or stop a behavior that causes another person distress. For instance, if a young child wants a toy that another child has, he takes it — by force if necessary. It takes a parent to guide him in understanding that there are four points of view that must be taken into account in this situation: his, the other child's, Mom's, and the other child's mom's. This is not inherent. It is learned. It is a stage of moral development that is beyond 2 years of age. So if a criminal takes what he wants — by force if necessary, and has no empathy for the person from whom he stole — then he is at this early 2-year-old stage of moral development. The question is: *Can he still develop morally beyond this 2-year-old stage? Or is he stuck there forever?* Although I am optimistic about treatment outcomes in some studies, the answer is *We do not yet know.* Perhaps future research will tell us more.

Attachment disordered youth have a negative view of themselves, are often upset with others, easily lose control of themselves, and have difficulty calming down. They were never taught the necessary life skills to be successful. Like the young boy, James, it is likely they were never sufficiently soothed, rocked, caressed, or kissed. When no one smiles at a baby, that baby will grow into an unsmiling adult.

How Attachment Disorders Affect Mind and Body

Secular psychology divorced itself from spirituality long ago, but recently, many theorists have been discussing how early abuse affects the child's sense of spirituality. We now understand that child physical and sexual abuse and neglect damage the child and the abuser in many ways, including spiritually (Madanes 1995). Spiritual injury can negatively affect drive and intuition. The survivor is unable to trust and form healthy relationships with a higher power or greater good, whatever he envisions that to be. While faith may require surrender of control, the abused or neglected survivor must attempt to be in control of his environment at all times because he feels the need to be constantly vigilant for danger from any source, even the unseen. He cannot surrender control of his life to a higher power that he cannot see and certainly cannot trust.

Abuse and neglect affect physical development as well. Research now shows that maltreated children have smaller brains than non-abused children (Perry and Pollard 1997). Often abused children have cognitive limitations, learning problems, and cognitive decline with increasing age. The neuro-chemicals for arousal are more easily induced in these children because of chronic states of excitement (Pollack 1998); this makes them get upset more easily and have a harder time calming down.

In the first three years of life, brain cells migrate from the primitive brain to the frontal cortex, and dendrites (neuronal functional connection sites) expand and multiply (Perry 1994). There are theories that rocking and sooth-ing of infants is necessary for adequate brain development. When the infant is neglected and does not experience these soothing actions from a caregiver, the result is a difficulty in processing complex information and feelings. A recent study (Gunn et al. 2006) found significant correlations between externalizing behavior problems (ADHD, ODD, aggressive and externalizing behaviors) and sensory deficits. They hypoth-esize that this may be an indication of a biological process or immature brain development. They also recommend that reducing the causes of sensory deficits in infancy has the potential to reduce externalizing behavior problems among children and adolescents. If, as others have suggested, the causes of immature brain development are severe abuse and neglect in infancy and early childhood, then eliminating that risk factor in infancy and early childhood is something we must address as a society.

Hare (1995) demonstrated these processing problems in his

study of psychopaths who were often abused and neglected. Adult psychopaths have deficient processing abilities in the pre-frontal cortex and areas of the brain that process emotion, such as the amygdyla. According to Hare, the state of hyper-arousal and interrupted brain development also interferes with learning and problem-solving. Psychopaths are poor in problem-solving, particularly if there is emotion involved. They do not learn from their mistakes, nor do they have normal fear responses.

Incidences of Child Maltreatment

- *In 2003 there were 3 million cases of child maltreatment (Gaudiosi 2004)*
- *The rate of reported child maltreatment in 2003 was 55 per 1,000 children in the U.S. (Gaudiosi 2004)*
- *In Canada in 2001, 22 per 1,000 children were reported to be maltreated (Trocme and Wolfe 2001).*

Chapter 2

Characteristics of Children with Disrupted Attachment Patterns

be careful as you go
cos little people grow
and little people know
when little people fight,
we may look easy pickings
but we got some bite!
so never kick a dog
because it's just a pup
you'd better run for cover when the pup grows up
and we'll fight like twenty armies
and we won't give up
~ Les Misérables

Charlie was a tall, thin, and handsome young man with a shock of blond hair as unruly as his personality. Although his appearance was agreeable, this 16-year-old's actions were anything but. Charlie was failing out of school. He bullied other kids and could never fully grasp the fact that his needs were not the only ones that existed or counted. He was the class clown, spoke out of turn, and showed little interest in learning. He was often on restriction for stealing from classmates. His poor scholastic performance was likely due to a previously undetected learning problem in reading, yet no one had ever taken the time to diagnose the disability or offer him extra help.

Why didn't his parents intervene to discipline and help their son? Because his violent, drug-addict mom and dad had abandoned Charlie and his little sister when they were 6 and 5 years old, respectively. As far as Charlie was concerned, he had no parents. He and his sister had been shuffled like used department store goods in and out of 11 foster homes. When I met Charlie, he was in a residential treatment center for molesting a younger child.

How did Charlie go from acting out in school to molesting another child? Was the former a precursor to the latter? Charlie made me wonder what the differences are between children who have anti-social behaviors and those who are pro-social, and how their past experiences determine their futures. In cases of children like Charlie, how can we prevent such a loss of human potential and protect the innocent people that lie in their dangerous paths?

In 1999 I started compiling a database to help me study the characteristics of a group of children with DAP, like Charlie. I looked at the common characteristics of youth with severe behavior problems. It started as a list to help me write my reports more efficiently, and burgeoned into a useful resource for my colleagues as well.

Disordered attachment was measured with the CARE Attachment Subscale (Seifert 2006). The sample (n=486) of youth with attachment problems is a subset of a larger sample (N=924) of children and adolescents that were administered the CARE (Child and Adolescent Risk Evaluation; Seifert 2003). In the sample with attachment problems, 41 percent were under the age of 13, 57 percent were between the ages of 13 and 18, and 2 percent were between the ages of 18 and 21. Sixty-six percent were male and 32 percent were female. Seventy percent had committed an assault. Fifty-four percent were Caucasian, 37 percent African American, 2 percent were Hispanic, and 6 percent were of other ethnic origin. Seventy percent were in the community and 30 percent were in a placement. Five percent had either no problems or mild ones, 93 percent had moderate to severe problems. Sixty-eight percent had average IQs.

All Children with DAP experienced early abuse or neglect or exposure to domestic violence. All youth had behavioral problems; 5 percent had mild problems, 2 percent had moderate problems, and 7 percent had severe behavior problems. Ninety-five percent had a history of severe behavior problems and assaults. Fifty-four percent of the group had committed more than three assaults (see Figure 2). It is important to note that there are disrupted attachment patterns that are not violent, but there has not been sufficient research to delineate these sub-types.

After extensive research, I discovered that there are significant relationships among family violence, youth violence, attachment problems, and the early childhood maltreatment (including severe neglect) of children. In Charlie's case, being exposed to violence and drugs at an extremely young age, combined with a lack of positive, constant mother and father figures in his life were enough. We cannot say that one caused the other, only that they are related somehow. Only future research will tell us the nature of the relationship and in what way certain variables — such as different methods of exposures to violence or level of success in school — interact and affect risk for violence. The study of these connections will, however, point the way to interventions that may prevent future youth violence.

A Theory of How Attachment Experiences May Affect Development

Abuse, trauma, neglect, caregiver unavailability, domestic violence, and resulting attachment problems can interrupt and interfere with a child's normal developmental processes and the ability to learn and practice important skills. One of these skills is the ability to manage emotions. Children with attachment problems experience little emotion, but when they do, they often do not understand it, know how to modulate it (that is, keep it from getting out of control), or express it appropriately. Moral development of children with DAP is another development area that is often dwarfed in comparison to that of pro-social children. They simply fail to comprehend and learn the "rules of society" and how to reciprocate with others (see Figure 2.1).

There is a predictable progression of moral development throughout one's lifetime. I will go into more detail on this in Chapter 3. In the early stages of moral development (birth to 2 years old), children believe that what is right is what meets the needs of the self. It appears that children with disrupted attachment patterns remain in this very early childhood stage of moral development. They are in the "Me, Me, Me!" stage and have not yet acknowledged that relationships, reciprocity, and membership in groups are important factors of life. Additionally, they lack empathy and show this by bullying, fighting, and being cruel to animals and smaller or younger children. Exercising power and cruelty over a helpless animal or smaller child can be an indicator of not having caring feelings about the welfare of other living beings (Levy and Orlans 1999).

In order to fully understand how attachment problems affect the normal developmental progression, one must understand that age alone is not the decisive factor in determining developmental level. One type of development may progress normally, while another is delayed. When development in one stage is hindered, problems will occur in later stages. Abuse, neglect, and trauma can delay development in one or more areas, while the bonding between child and caregiver supports healthy growth.

We've all seen people in this early stage of development. Teenagers who only care about their own needs — *I want the pink cell phone with rhinestones that costs more than all the others... now! I want to be the best football player on the field and I don't care who I have to hurt to get there!* Until they master this stage, they cannot move to the next. They must learn to see things from another person's perspective (e.g. that of their mothers, their fathers, or their peers), which is a more mature level of moral and relationship skill development.

In the next chapter, we will examine the normal and disturbed characteristics of the Six Stages of Moral Development. I will offer several infamous examples to help illustrate how Kohlberg's theory applies to youth with and without attachment problems.

Chapter 3

The Six Stages of Moral Development

By 1971, Lawrence Kohlberg and Elliot Turiel were able to determine the Six Stages of Moral Development, which begin at birth and continue into adulthood. In each stage there are developmental tasks to be accomplished. Kohlberg describes appropriate and dysfunctional child-rearing environments for the early age groups; each will either support or interfere with the development of skills at the proceeding stages. Attachment is the basis for learning interpersonal skills, emotional regulation, and problem-solving abilities and is a primary characteristic of an appropriate child-rearing environment.

In the following pages I examine three notorious serial killers and one criminal mastermind. I find it important not only to note their crimes, but also to observe their childhoods — where the roots of their evil were encouraged to grow, however unknowingly, by those around them. Their interrupted, miserable childhoods, as well as numerous warning signs that went unheeded by family and correctional authorities cannot be discounted as primary factors for their later actions, violent as they were. Each criminal is an extreme example of what can go wrong when skill development is hindered and

attachments disrupted. While some worry that this will allow criminals to escape taking responsibility for their behavior, this book is
really about the prevention of future dangerous behaviors.

Moral Developmental Stage I
Infants & Toddlers — Birth to 2 Years Old

Case Study: Theodore Kaczynski, AKA The Unabomber

As an adult, Theodore Kaczynski was not yet at an adult stage of moral or social development. Intellectually brilliant but socially inept,
he was a hermit who could not cooperate with others, and did not
acquire skills learned in the first stage of moral development. Known
now in infamy as the Unabomber (the University and Airline Bomber),
Kaczynski did not feel guilt or remorse for killing and maiming over
30 people — he felt that his belief system justified harming others
(Serial Killer Crime Index). He never fully understood or practiced
reciprocity.

Kaczynski was born in 1942 in Chicago. Due to a hospitalization, he
had very little contact with his parents for a short period of time
during his infancy. According to his mother, he was never the same
afterwards (Ottley 2006). (I suspect this time, marked by a lack of
motherly love, cradling, and caressing may have weighed heavily on
Kaczynski's later issues.) She said that he was not involved in any
sports or other peer group activities, and reported that Ted engaged
in parallel play as a child yet never continued on to interactive play.
She considered having him assessed for autism, but did not do so
(Johnson 1998). Kaczynski's little brother, David, did not endure a
similar hospitalization, and from all accounts but Kaczynski's, the

Kaczynski parents were loving and supportive. However, Kaczynski claimed in his court evaluation that he was emotionally and verbally abused as a child. If Kaczynski does indeed have an untreated autism spectrum, schizophrenia, or other disorder, then this would explain — though not excuse — much of his behavior.

Kaczynski was regarded as a genius. As a child and teenager, he skipped grades in school and was accepted to Harvard at the age of 16. Yet the aloof young man was never able to make friends or be accepted into a peer group; his classmates teased him for being different.

While a student at Harvard, Kaczynski was given a psychological examination in the form of a Thematic Apperception Test (TAT). The TAT is a projective test of personality developed by Christiana D. Morgan and Henry A. Murray in the 1930s at the Harvard Psychological Clinic. The TAT from Kaczynski's examination had never been scored back at Harvard, but Dr. Karen Froming (Johnson 1998; *http://www.courttv.com/trials/unabomber/documents/psychological.html*) later did so during the course of his murder trial. She concluded that Kaczynski would have been diagnosed as a paranoid schizophrenic at that time. It appeared that he was depressed and distressed about not having a female companion. He sought therapy on a few occasions, but did not follow through with services. He took Trazodone, an antidepressant, for a few days and then discontinued the medication.

Kaczynski graduated from Harvard and went on to attain a master's degree and Ph.D. in Mathematics from the University of Michigan, Ann Arbor. He mystified colleagues and made a name for himself in the field of geometric function theory.

In his writings, Kaczynski expressed having anger at non-accep-
tance and bullying by peers, having violent fantasies, and wanting
revenge on those that had deeply hurt him. While at the University
of Michigan, he had concerns about needing a sex change operation
to become a female. His writings describe paranoia, noise sensitivity, isolation, fears of society trying to control his mind, suicidality,
homocidality, and rage. He went to a psychiatrist, but left in shame
and anger without discussing his fears and feelings. He later worked
for two years as a college professor at the University of California,
Berkley, and was still unable to build rapport with peers or students.
At that time, he planned to earn enough money to go into the woods,
live off the land, and kill the people he hated.

In 1971, the Kaczynski brothers bought land in Montana where Ted
Kaczynski moved into a very small, stark cabin in the woods. There
are reports that during his time in Montana he would steal and
destroy neighbors' property if they angered him. Also during this
time, Kaczynski held a variety of low-level, temporary, and part-time
jobs. Of particular interest is an incident that occurred 1978 — after Kaczynski had several dates with a woman he worked with, she
decided not to see him anymore. He became rageful to the point of
having fantasies of killing her and cutting her up. He was fired from
this job due to inappropriate behavior toward this woman. A thorough
psychological assessment of Kaczynski at this time would likely have
revealed his psychiatric problems and his need for treatment.

While there is no known evidence of substance abuse, Kaczynski's
family describes periods where Kaczynski was non-responsive to anyone for hours at a time. As he spent less and less time with his family,
in 1978 he sent the first of 16 letter bombs, which killed three and

injured 29. After an investigation that spanned almost two decades (the most expensive the FBI has ever conducted), Kaczynski was arrested in 1996.

During the initial stages of the trial, Kaczynski refused to place his sanity at issue. Later, he agreed to be examined by a mental health expert, Dr. Sally Johnson, who found him competent to stand trial. While on trial, Kaczynski attempted to hang himself in his cell. He was eventually convicted, and he now lives in a cell larger than his isolated cabin in the woods. Kaczynski, whose actions reflect a lack of empathy for others, had much anger toward his family and indiscriminate, inappropriate, and superficial affection toward a few women he barely knew. To Kaczynski, society controlled everything and he had to fight to keep from being destroyed. He exhibited many characteristics of someone with one or more of the following: attachment problems, paranoid schizophrenia, psychopathy, or an autism spectrum disorder. All amounted to the inability to see things from another person's point of view.

If Kaczynski's claims of child abuse are true, then it might help explain why he became violent, since mental illness alone is usually not sufficient for someone to become violent.

*   *   *

Infants and toddlers from birth to 2 years old have to be taught that objects exist even when they cannot be seen. They drop things repeatedly and delight when they reappear out of nowhere. Ever play peek-a-boo with an elated child? This game is more than laughs; it's actually teaching an important concept about the state of being. If a child is severely neglected and not exposed to these very normal interactions, these and other concepts may either be distorted or go unlearned.

A normally developing infant will cling to Mom and experience anxiety about being approached by strangers. It is an extremely dependent relationship with no boundaries between mother and child. If she protects the child from danger, then a trusting bond will develop between the two. It's a pattern for survival. If the child is not protected, the infant will not develop trust for caregivers or anxiety toward strangers as a survival strategy. Therefore many children with DAP have indiscriminant affection toward strangers and an indifference or even hatred toward their caregivers. They'll ask a stranger to take them home because they haven't developed stranger anxiety or the fear of being separated from a primary caregiver. Relationships are often very superficial.

During infancy, the child begins the process of incorporation through the sensory-perceptual systems. "If normal development proceeds, these incorporative experiences are mostly hedonic, psychologically gratifying, and physiologically stabilizing" (Meloy 2001). Sensory-perceptual systems are the basis for infants' and toddlers' ability to develop psychological structures and sensory integration during this very rapid period of growth. The emotions of anger and fear are forming rapidly, and can easily be seen from the day of birth. Babies who are hungry or want their mothers show their discontent by crying and screaming. As Bowlby taught us, this is a normal, instinctive behavior that brings the caregiver close when the infant is in need or in danger. It facilitates the infant/caregiver bond.

Between ages 1 and 2, children will start to show the first signs of independence from parents as they roll around, crawl, and get up and walk to explore their world. Mother is a safehaven from which the child may venture to explore the world and return to when frightened or in danger — another basic survival skill. The mother's reciprocal physical and emotional nurturing are essential for the brain to develop normally, especially in the areas that control language, process curiosity, and affect regulation. For many children with DAP, these areas of the brain have not developed sufficiently; thus many have borderline IQs, language difficulties, and learning problems.

This early stage of moral development is characterized by the commitment to self, the ME, ME, ME! stage in which Kaczynski was trapped. In more appropriate conditions, children are taught lessons such as what is good is rewarded, and what is bad is punished. Yet those, like Kaczynski, who miss this lesson internally think, *What is important is that I get my own needs met.* If there was disruption in the early stages of development — by abandonment, absence of a parent, neglect, abuse, or sexual molestation — the child may not formulate this concept of reward/punishment. As adults, although their bodies are developed, their psyche remains trapped in this early stage where satisfying their needs is primary and avoiding punishment is secondary. The internalized need to follow rules is absent, so they often choose immediate gratification over long-term gains. They are unable to respond to or respect social and moral boundaries. It is a fact that youth with antisocial traits, adult sociopaths, and psychopaths are not as responsive to reward and punishment as other adults.

On the other hand, children in this early stage of development with normal attachment patterns hardly seem to recognize that viewpoints differ. They assume that there is only one right view — that of authorities and the "big people" who control everything. Since their relationship with the caregiver is totally dependent, the child does not distinguish between caregiver and self. Older children with disrupted attachment patterns assume that there is only one point of view (their own) because big people are either absent or mean and abusive, and therefore cannot be trusted. Learning at this stage is the basis for all later moral development and relationship patterns (Kohlberg and Turiel 1971); disruption will distort or thwart future moral and social development.

Moral Developmental Stage II
Early Childhood — 2 to 7 Years Old

Case Study: Charles Manson

The name Charles Manson has been synonomous with evil ever since the multiple Tate and LaBianca murders, which Manson ordered, took place in 1969.

Manson was born to a teenage mother who became both an alcoholic and prostitute, and he never had a stable father figure. His whole life is characterized by conduct disorder, sociopathy, and the inability to experience guilt. He was extremely manipulative and had spent more than half his life in institutions (Bardsley 2006). It is likely that Manson did not morally mature past the early childhood stage.

Manson's mother was often absent and irresponsible; little Charlie was constantly passed from one substitute caregiver to the next and from one institution to the next. Manson reported that his mother once sold him to a waitress for a pitcher of beer. Manson began to steal and was eventually sent to Boys Town, a treatment facility that cares for abused, abandoned, and neglected children. While there he committed two armed robberies and was then sent to the Indiana School for Boys. Those who came in contact with Manson described him as unable to trust in anyone. After escaping and carrying out a string of armed robberies, he was sent to the National Training School for Boys, where he sodomized another boy while holding a razor to his throat. He was moved to a more secure facility where he made some progress, and was paroled in 1954. In time, he went back to prison.

Prison officials described Manson as having a tremendous need to call negative attention to himself. "He hides his resentment and hostility behind a mask of superficial ingratiation," a prison official reported in court documents, "...even his cries for help represent a desire for attention with only superficial meaning." Once out of prison in the late 1960s, he gathered around him a group of emotionally unstable and dependent young women, whom he manipulated with charm and drugs. Later known as "The Family," they lived out of trash cans in San Francisco and then Southern California, whilst Manson hoped to become famous with his music.

Manson was introduced to record producer Terry Melcher through the Beach Boys' Dennis Wilson, and went to his Beverly Hills mansion to audition for a contract. After Melcher denied Manson a record deal, Manson later ordered his followers to return to the site and kill all who occupied the house. At that time, director Roman Polanski and actress Sharon Tate were living on the premises, and although Manson knew the property was inhabited by new people, he ordered the senseless killing anyway. One theory for a motive was that the location represented Manson's rejection by the show business community he wanted to enter, and that it was of no interest to him who his actual victims would be. Still another possible reason for the murder of Tate, her unborn child, and four others is that Manson hoped it would ignite a race war if authorties believed African Americans killed this group of Caucasians.

Manson and The Family also killed Leno LaBianca, a supermarket senior manager, and his wife Rosemary. Charles tied up the victims and then returned to the car after giving the command to his followers to kill them. Mrs. LaBianca was stabbed 41 times and Mr. LaBianca was found with a carving fork sticking out of his stomach and the word "WAR" carved into his body. These senseless murders are described in the book, *Helter Skelter* (Bugliosi and Gentry 1974).

Manson and several members of The Family were imprisoned for life for these murders. In parole hearings, Manson still rages at the unfairness of his imprisonment. We know he was at a stage of development where he could form some relationships because of his "family" of followers, yet his rage, a desire for revenge (a typical symptom of those with disrupted attachment patterns), and lack of remorse seem to be more important to him than following the rules of society (Bardsley and Marilyn).

*   *   *

The early developmental stage taking place between ages 2 and 7 marks a time when children's bodies and brains are growing rapidly. Their large and small muscles expand and they become better coordinated. At this age level, children are very active and have short attention spans. Their thinking is still self-centered. Language develops quickly if they are exposed to others communicating. If they are not, the language area of the brain will undergo some pruning, which often causes later language and communication problems among children and teens with DAP.

A healthy youth in the early childhood stage feels guilty about his misbehavior and feels ashamed when he fails. Similarly, a child at an older age who remains in this stage of moral development because of a conduct disorder, may not experience guilt. An abnormal youth may feel bad if he gets caught doing something mischievous — but only because he doesn't like the negative consequences of his actions, not because he feels guilt. Such people, like Manson, have yet to graduate this stage of development, in which they feel true guilt or empathy for others.

A 2- to 7-year-old is able to start things on his own initiative. He seeks approval and relationships with his parents, teachers, and peers, but is also primarily concerned with his own needs. A child in this stage will obey rules to avoid punishment and will develop the ability to play cooperatively. This is when the understanding of reciprocity, the basis of human cooperation, blossoms. *You scratch my back and I'll scratch yours.*

"Commitment to relationships" is the overarching theme to this second stage of moral development. Children recognize that people have different interests and viewpoints. They seem to be overcoming egocentrism; they see that perspectives are relative to the individual. They also start to consider how individuals might coordinate their interests in terms of mutually beneficial deals. Adults with severe Borderline or Narcissistic Personality disorders, again, like Manson, likely have not reached the reciprocity stage of moral development. They are able to manipulate others to get their needs met, but do not really care about other people's needs.

If you are a therapist, then think for a moment about the teenagers with whom you work who are either not yet at or are only in this stage of development. Asking them to perform a developmental task associated with an adolescent stage of moral or social development when they are still in an early childhood stage is like expecting Average Joe to climb Mount Everest or fly an airplane. They're just not ready and must be taught the earlier skills in sequence to bring them to age-appropriate skills. Children who have experienced disruptions that have affected the earlier stages of development, unless provided appropriate interventions, will continue to have disturbances in the later developmental stages.

Moral Developmental Stage III
Middle Childhood — 7 to 11 Years Old

Case Study: David Berkowitz, AKA Son of Sam

David Berkowitz, born in 1953 and known in infamy as Son of Sam, was given up by his biological mother at infancy and adopted by new parents. Although his new parents took excellent care of him, and by no means is adoption necessarily a precursor to violence, Berkowitz went on to lead a troubled childhood. He took to petty larceny and pyromania and, although he loved to play baseball, was known in his Queens neighborhood as a bully. He never received adequate treatment for mental health problems as a child. In the late 1970s, Berkowitz went on to kill six people — wounding and paralyzing many others using a .44 caliber Charter Arms Bulldog. His actions show that he never accomplished middle childhood development.

Berkowitz's adoptive mother died of breast cancer when he was a teenager, and when his adoptive dad married another woman, he was extremely distraught. His dad relocated to Florida with his new bride and left his son to his own devices in 1971. Berkowitz created what was, for him, a very realistic fantasy life to replace his forlorn real life. For comfort and to show that he still had control over some things, he set nearly 1500 fires across New York City and kept a diary of it. He wrote to his father of his despair while his mental health continued to deteriorate. From there, he said, "the demons" took over, and one such demon — in the form of his neighbor's black Labrador retriever — told him to begin his killing spree.

The murders began near the apartment that he shared with his father after his mother died. The victims were mostly young women with long brown hair and couples sitting in their cars late at night. Berkowitz later claimed that pornography and his membership to a satanic cult influenced his deeds. While a court-ordered psychiatric evaluation gave him the diagnosis of paranoid schizophrenia, he was found competent to stand trial. After he was found guilty and sentenced to 365 years in jail, Berkowitz confessed in an interview to FBI veteran Robert Ressler that the demon story was fake. He stated that the killings were revenge for abandonment by his mother and for him not having relationships with women. He became aroused by stalking and killing women and masturbated afterwards. When he couldn't find a victim, he would return to the scenes of earlier crimes to masturbate.

Although he now claims from his prison cell — where he is serving six consecutive life sentences — that he is a born-again Christian, Berkowitz, who confessed to the murders, had no empathy for his victims. His whole life he failed to develop the ability to form deep relationships with other people. His needs were more important than those of others. Is his current claim to born-again Christianity and redemption to be taken at face value? It is doubtful.

*   *   *

Attention span lengthens during normal middle childhood development, from ages 7 to 11. This third stage of moral development is characterized by commitment to the immediate or local group and social quid pro quo, and yet one's own needs are still the most important. Youths in middle childhood conceptualize role-taking as a deeper, more empathic process when one becomes concerned with the other's feelings. Those who lack empathy and the ability to form relationship attachments have not yet entered or completed this stage of development.

A youth with DAP may be very self-involved and not have an understanding of fair deals, or reciprocation, because the earlier concept of giving/getting has not been accomplished. Bowlby (1944) theorized that a pattern of detachment caused by continuous maternal rejection was associated with a typology he called "affectionless psychopathy." This describes quite sufficiently Berkowitz's condition, having been first rejected by his biological mother, followed by the death of his adoptive mother and the abandonment by his father when he moved to Florida. For children still mastering earlier stages of development involving immediate gratification, a longer attention span is not mastered and the child remains disorganized and impulsive.

Thus many children with DAP are impulsive and disorganized. They suffer from delays in understanding the concepts of time and space. Not having a model of positive relationships, their relationships with peers will remain superficial — if developed at all. Because peer approval is so important, rejection by peers and adults can push a youth toward deviant behaviors or destructive peer alternatives. Additionally, if learning at this middle development stage is disrupted, then an understanding of moral rules won't begin. Self-confidence may fall to the wayside. This would explain Berkowitz's sad tale of rejection by family and a life of bullying and violence.

Moral Developmental Stage IV Adolescence — 11 to 18 Years Old

Case Study: Ted Bundy

Ted Bundy is the poster child of the American serial killer. With his handsome looks and cool demeanor, he wooed, tricked, and outright ambushed dozens of women in order to fulfill his sick fantasies. Bundy finally confessed to killing 30 women — although he was suspected of having up to 100 victims — and sent to the electric chair. This charismatic, psychopathic killer was never remorseful for his misdeeds, which leads me to believe that he never passed the adolescent stage of moral development. While Bundy had some characteristics of this stage, such as logistical thinking, his self-centered views and lack of empathy show he may not have mastered earlier moral stages either. Thus Bundy had a mix of several developmental stages, demonstrating that one part of development (cognitive) can advance quite normally, while others (interpersonal and moral) can lag far behind.

Bundy was born into an unstable and confused family environ-ment. Due to his mother's unwed teenage status, he was raised by his grandparents and believed his mother was his older sister. His grandfather was mentally erratic and violent. It is alleged that on several occasions, young Ted arranged knives at his aunt's bed-side. This sort of hostile nighttime display is not uncommon among children with severe attachment problems — they sometimes roam the house at night and have a need to control others by using fear. The idea is "I will show you how vulnerable you are, so you will not attack or try to harm or control me." When his mother got older she remarried, and around this time, Bundy discovered that the woman he thought to be his sister was in fact his mother. Bundy had a very hard time coping with all of the sudden changes in his life — not only the realization about his true mother, but also getting a new stepfather at the same time.

As a youth, Bundy was shy and awkward, and he didn't seem to un-derstand the reasons for or mechanisms of interpersonal relationships (Bell 2006). In middle school, he was the victim of bullies. By high school, he was superficially social and gregarious. He was reported to be a compulsive thief, shoplifter, and amateur conman — as well as a neighborhood peeping Tom.

Although a good student in high school, as an adult, Bundy had a spotty work record. Due to his immaturity, he failed to fit in while attending college. He became obsessed with his first love even after she broke up with him. He was devastated and dropped out of school, — eventually taking revenge on her by manipulating her into falling in love with him again, proposing marriage, and then rejecting her without warning or explanation. While it is suspected that the earliest of his murders occurred when Bundy was 15, his first known killing took place when he was 27 (Bell 2006). It was to mark the beginning of a murder spree that would last four years, spanning from Washington State to Utah to Florida. Eventually tried and convicted of multiple murders, he was executed in 1989.

It is important to remember that despite his horrible actions, Bundy, like many psychopaths, was intelligent, attractive, and charming. Bundy represented himself at his own trial; the judge stated that had circumstances been otherwise, Bundy would have made an excellent attorney because of his cool, persuasive speaking and charm. It's no wonder how psychopaths fool others into thinking that they are ordinary people with good intentions — others how they lure their prey into their deadly clutches.

* * *

Despite what parents may think, adolescents can reason in logical ways — at least some of the time. When children are between the ages 11 and 18, in this fourth stage of moral development also known as adolescence, children learn the importance of group membership and the Golden Rule. They learn that morality is based on intentions rather than outcome. For many teens, peer approval is more important than adult approval, and they often resist conforming to adult standards. This fact may be similar for all teens, but each expresses his own rebellion differently. For youth with disrupted attachment patterns who have not completely left the stage of egocentricity, such as Bundy, this new stage of moral development cannot be successfully mastered.

Many attachment-disturbed youth have delays in their ability to think logically and solve problems. Those with normal development are able to feel remorse, while those with DAP are either limited or lack the facility to feel remorse or empathy for others. While normally developing teens try to formulate a sense of identity, this is more difficult for those with attachment problems because their sense of identity is not based in reality. The internal working model is one of the "bad seed." Many people begin sexual relationships during teenage years; for youth with attachment problems, these relationships and ones built later in life will remain superficial and for the purposes of self-gratification and manipulation. For Bundy, who engaged in necrophilia, sex was the ultimate example of self-gratification because he did not have to have a relationship with his "partner." Though Bundy had several relationships with women that lasted several years, they were all just outlets for his manipulations.

Moral Developmental Stages V — VI Adulthood

For those who have had secure attachments in childhood, the last two stages of moral development are accomplished in adulthood.

- Stage V — *Commitment to greater society*. One accepts that rules and social contracts maintain the social order. There is a broader, society-wide conception of how people coordinate their roles through the legal system. *Laws are for the greatest good to the most people.* Morals are less black and white. Democratic processes are accepted as rule. Stage V exemplifies most pro-social adults, such as many of you reading this book. This stage has not been mastered by sociopathic and psychopathic individuals.

- Stage VI — *Self-chosen ethical principles — understanding the universal principles of fairness and justice.* Stage VI considers how all parties take one another's perspectives according to the principles of justice. It is a more idealized look at how people might coordinate their interests. This stage is reserved for the great leaders of the world such as Gandhi, Abraham Lincoln, Nelson Mandela, and Martin Luther King.

Adults establish their social framework by starting families and/or careers. To successfully do so, they must have a sound ability to form positive social relationships. Those with personality disorders, criminals, the mentally ill, and those who have problems with violence, sexual offenses, and substance abuse have less well-developed relationship skills.

After examining the stories of these four psychopathic criminals, we can see how attachment problems in early childhood can disrupt the normal progression of moral development stages. Each shows how attachment and personality disordered adults appear to be at earlier stages of moral-development. While each of these examples is extreme, violence occurs on many levels in the United States.

In 1990, Dr. Kim Bartholomew studied attachment problems in adulthood. She found that those with the dismissing type of attachment view themselves as positive and others as negative. Those with this type of attachment problem distance themselves from others. The typology has been associated with conduct disorder and Antisocial Personality Disorder (Allen, Hauser, and Borman-Spurrell 1996). Raine, Brennan, and Mednick (1994, 1997) found that early onset of violence before age 18 was correlated with birth complications and maternal rejection in the first year of life. Hare and Neuman (2005) also found that patterns of hypo-arousal (perhaps a result of chronic under-stimulation in infancy) in psychopaths contributed to the inability to respond to punishment in the same way that non-psychopaths do, inhibiting their ability to learn from their mistakes.

Chapter 4

Why Do People Resort to Violence?

I can't help but cringe every time I hear on the news about another father or mother killing his or her children, children killing classmates or parents, or shootings of bosses and coworkers in the workplace. Many people ask, *What's wrong with these people? Why is there so much violence in our world?*

The United States has greater rates of both youth and general violence than any other Western nation (Commission on Behavioral and Social Sciences and Education 1993). There are many theories for this high rate of violence. Children and teens experience violence at home, at school, and in the community, and they replicate what they see in their own actions. Some think that the use of corporal and other harsh punishments in the U.S. is to blame. Others place responsibility on the extremely violent media such as the video game *Grand Theft Auto*. Then there is the abundance of guns and the laws that protect their widespread ownership. Yet others state that our strong value on personal independence makes us reluctant to interfere with how parents raise their children, even when it is violent or neglectful.

But violence takes place all over the world as well. In the Middle East, Asia, South America, Africa, and Europe, wars have ravaged families and orphaned children for centuries. We want to know why violence happens so that we can try to make some sense of it all.

Chart 1 — The Following Images Are Etched into our Memories Forever:

- In 2005, Colorado woman drowned her two small children and then made a heart-wrenching plea on the news for their return.
- In 1998, a 17-year-old killed his mother and then went on a shooting rampage at his Mississippi high school.
- Also in 1998, two kids, one 13 and the other 11, killed four classmates and one teacher in Jonesboro, Arkansas.
- In the 1990s, the Menendez brothers killed their parents and later reported years of sexual abuse by their father.
- Two young males murdered 13 teens and teachers and then committed suicide in the 1999 Columbine High School massacre in Littleton, Colorado.
- A month after Columbine, a 15-year-old gunned down six people in a Georgia school.
- There have been at least two other teenage plots to replicate the Columbine massacre.
- In 2005, a student at Red Lake High in Minnesota killed seven people and then himself.
- In 1995, Timothy McVeigh and Terry Nichols detonated a large truck bomb outside the Morrow Federal Building in Oklahoma City, killing 168 people, including office workers and children in the ground-floor nursery.

Chart 2 — U.S. Youth and Family Violence Statistics

- Homicide has been the leading cause of death among African Americans age 15 to 34 since 1978 (U.S. Dept. of Health and Human Services 2001).

- In 2003, an average of 15 young people per day were murdered (CDC Youth Violence Fact Sheet).

- According to NCVS, women with the lowest annual income ($7,500 and below) had a rate of interpersonal violence seven times that of women in the highest income category ($75,000 and above) (Family Violence Prevention Fund).

- One in 10 youths witnesses a stabbing or shooting every year (CDC Youth Violence Statistics).

- The rate of child homicide by firearm in the United States is 16 times greater than in a number of other western industrialized countries such as England, France, and Germany combined (Snyder and Sickmund September 1999).

- There were 28,663 firearm deaths in the U.S. in 2000. Of that figure, 11,071 (39 percent) were homicides (including 270 deaths from police action). These rates are by far the highest in the industrialized world (CDC Youth Violence Fact Sheet).

We can begin to understand violence by looking at its roots in childhood. The Causes and Correlates Program (Kelly et al. 1997) has collected data on juvenile violence trends in the U.S. since 1986. This study followed over 4,000 juveniles in three sites for over two decades. The study drew the following conclusions about juveniles:

1. Childhood maltreatment is associated with later behavior problems. Maltreatment doubles the risk that a youth will have multiple problems.

2. Less serious behavior problems precede more serious forms of delinquency. There is a term, Persistent Severe Violence, which describes a pattern of disruptive behaviors that begin in preschool and last through adulthood with increasing severity. The earlier that severe behavior problems are seen, the more likely that a life course pattern of serious delinquency will begin unless appropriate intervention takes place.

3. Serious delinquents have co-occurring problems, such as substance abuse, learning problems, and mental illness.

4. Very young children sometimes commit violent acts. Problem behaviors often begin before the age of 13. Some juveniles committed serious violent acts at as young as 10 years of age.

5. Violence among girls has increased.

6. Early intervention, which frequently is not employed, is the best method of redirecting the emerging negative behaviors of aggressive children. Well-tested risk assessments are avail-

able (please see Part II for assessments).

What does this mean? The researchers suggest:

- Do not dismiss early warning signs of disruptive behaviors.
- Victims of maltreatment should be identified and treated early.
- All adults who are responsible for children in some way must come together to protect, screen, and treat youths at risk.

Adult male violence is often associated with past acts of violence, sexual violence, difficulty with bonding, and the combination of mental illness and substance abuse. The relationship of mental illness to substance abuse and increased violence was also a finding of the MacArthur study (Monahan et al. 2001), and Hare (1995) found that psychopathy is highly related to repeat violence against others.

Drew Ross (1998) describes the histories and lives of several murderers and rapist murderers. He portrays histories of childhood neglect, horrible abuse, devastating domestic violence, and the resultant rage. It is clear that some murderers re-enact childhood traumas where love, hate, sex, and violence are intertwined in a matrix of macabre, twisted thoughts and actions. Violent persons have significant histories of maltreatment in childhood and evidence of attachment problems that date back to early childhood. As Ross states, this theory is not meant to coddle inmates who have done horrible things — which always seems to be a worry for some — but to understand the deep and devastating roots of violence. With increased understanding of violence and prevention strategies, it is possible to decrease the number of violent crimes around the world.

Dorothy Otnow Lewis (1998) observed and studied violent youth and found that a combination of horrific abuse and neglect, school failure, poor anger management skills, neurological damage, drug and alcohol use, and lack of effective treatment were the ingredients for teenage violence.

Chart 3 — Crime Index Offense Clock (Department of Justice, Federal Bureau of Investigation)

In the United States:
- *There is one Crime Index Offense every 2.7 seconds.*
- *Every 22.1 seconds there is one violent crime.*
- *Every 35.3 seconds there is one aggravated assault.*
- *Every 1.2 minutes there is one robbery.*
- *Every 5.5 minutes there is one forcible rape.*
- *Every 32.4 minutes there is one murder.*

Gangs

In the United States, there are approximately 31,000 gangs in 4,800 jurisdictions. At the turn of the 20th century, gangs were primarily young immigrant groups who were attached to their community, culture, and each other. They engaged in aging activities that were for the purposes of turf protection, power, and economic gain. This can be seen in the movie, *Gangs of New York* (Miramax 2002). Some gangs today have similar characteristics. For instance, many Hispanic gangs in Los Angeles are closely tied to the barrio and are turf-oriented. Juvenile gang members are responsible for a large percentage of youth violence nationwide.

The risk factors for gang membership are similar to the risk factors for youth violence in general. It would seem logical that these are vulnerable, unsupervised youth looking for a peer group who are not on a pro-social path to success. They are drawn to the chance for status, social networks, and the "success" that a gang (from their perspective) can provide.

Chart 4 — Strongest Longitudinal Risk Factors for Gang Membership:

- *Lack of social attachment to the community*
- *Low parental attachment to the child*
- *Low parental supervision of child*
- *Low expectations for school success*
- *Low commitment to school*
- *Low attachment to teachers*
- *Delinquent peers*
- *Negative life events*
- *Drug use and violent delinquency*

The greater the number of risk factors (seven-plus) experienced in the pre-teen years, the higher the risk of gang involvement (Howell 1998).

The majority of gang violence is either within or between gangs. In some gangs, violence is seen as a display of machismo that bonds members to the group and brings them status within the group. It is also a means of controlling the group; it is used for rivalry, revenge, and to gain favor or advantage. Although homicides committed by gangs are down in number, a member of a youth gang is 60 times more likely to be killed than a youth in the general population.

Some gangs have migrated from cities to suburban and rural areas. Well-known gangs include the Crips, Bloods, Latin Kings, Black Gangster Disciples, Asian Boyz, East Coast Gang, Mara Salvatrucha or MS-13, and Folk Nation Gang. The most dangerous gang in America today is MS-13, which originated in El Salvador. They have 8,000 to 10,000 members in 33 states in the U.S. and tens of thousands in Central America. MS-13 is an adult gang with adolescent members. There is a large concentration of MS-13 groups in Northern Virginia, and they are spreading rapidly. They specialize in both human and drug trafficking, robbery, extortion, rape, and murder.

MS-13 was formed by El Salvadorians fleeing the war and torture common in parts of Central America. They sought to find a place to reside among the city streets of Los Angeles, which were already populated by Crips and Bloods and other territorial gangs. Organizing in groups meant survival — Mara means posse and salvatruchas means street tough Salvadorians, and the number 13 is linked with Southern California. Many members came from broken families and had been exposed to violence throughout their lives. Organizing groups was essential for survival in such hostile environments.

MS-13 very clearly shows a trajectory of a group of children and families who were exposed to violence, broken apart, and dropped in a hostile, violent environment. They became as violent and anti-social as the environment they left and the ones they moved to — the underpinnings of pro-social development were disrupted and unsupported. "Dissing" or "ratting on" a MS-13 member can result in being hacked to death with machetes, and initiations into the gang are also violent. Youths who have become disconnected from their communities, families, schools, and pro-social peers are vulnerable to be pulled into this and other gangs.

There are things parents can do to help keep their kids out of gangs and other unwanted activities:

- Talk to your child.
- Know who your child's friends are. Meet his friends and their parents.
- Know where your pre-teens and adolescents are and what they are doing.
- Set up fair, reasonable rules with natural consequences. Make sure your kid knows the rules, rewards, and consequences and that he sticks to them.
- Make sure positive statements to your child outnumber negative statements by a ratio of at least four to one.
- Organize a community watch and coordinate with the police.
- If your child's behavior changes in a negative way (e.g. grades drop, he becomes oppositional, is never home, has erratic behavior, sleeps too much or too little) check into it. Don't ignore it — find out what is going on.
- Talk to your child's teachers.
- Plan family activities.
- Although your lives may be hectic these days, eat and talk together at least a few times a week (Howell 1998).

Characteristics of Violent Cults

Violent cults follow the same patterns already discussed. In fact, it appears that cult leaders know how to gain control of their flock by using rigid routines, being non-tolerant of actions from the rules, practicing corporal punishment for the smallest infractions in rituals, and sexually abusing children. From Jim Jones to Warren Jeffs, the overarching ideas are the same. Why would logical people follow such obviously mentally unstable and cruel leaders?

Generally, cults are run by psychopaths. Psychopaths are known for their tremendous charisma, their lack of concern for the needs of others, and their need to control people. These (mostly) men target vulnerable people who are looking for a place or group where they feel they belong. Many of these vulnerable people grew up abused, neglected, abandoned, and exposed to violence. Consequently, their ability to distinguish the "good guys" from the "bad guys" is often upside-down (trust the one you shouldn't and don't trust the ones you should). Their ability to bond appropriately may be compromised — they may be indiscriminately affectionate (a symptom of attachment problems) and/or closed off emotionally to those who care about and try to help them. Once entrenched in the cult, where brainwashing techniques are deliberately used, it is very difficult for them to free themselves.

Another problem with cults is their closed systems. Systems are groups of parts, entities, people, etc. that work together for a goal. Families, universities, and cities are examples of systems. Information travels in and out of that system to and from other systems.

A family gets information from the school, TV, or community, for example they may give information to another family or neighbor. A university gets information from other universities, the Internet, and books, and vice versa. Information goes in and out of the system on a continuum from extremely closed to extremely open. In cults, there is often conflict, communication, and cooperation to a greater or lesser degree within their closed system. As with most things, the extremes are not healthy. The more closed a system is, the less healthy it will be. A closed system will restrict information, to a greater degree, from going into or out of its organization. Organizational information is not updated and there is little or no change or growth. Rules, relationships, and the environment become distorted or dysfunctional without feedback from the outside world to correct itself.

Cult leaders often keep their communities closed in order to keep out other influences. This encourages members to evaluate the culture or group "rules" without objectivity. Of course, cult leaders deliberately make it this way so that the members will not recognize that what is happening is wrong, and if they do, they will be too afraid to speak up.

My Cult Investigation

There is much controversy about ritualized child abuse and sacrifices by organized cults. I quite easily found one such cult on the internet called the Order of the Nine Black Angels (Wikipedia - http://en.wikipedia.org/wiki/Order_of_Nine_Angels). There are links to their site that discuss ritual abuse and human sacrifice. While researching this topic, I also came across articles stating that there is no known evidence of the ritual abuse of children by satanic cults. So I did a little investigating on my own.

I went to a place rumored to be a haven where people have performed satanic rituals. The rooms were dark. The walls were covered in primitive, bizarre paintings depicting skeletons, fires, boxes with blood dripping from them, strange writing, odd designs, and indecipherable writing. Straw or hay covered the floor. My heart raced and I felt as if someone was watching me. I wanted to vomit, even though there was no stench — only the smell of hay weighing me down.

I have also spoken with several people said that they were ritually abused by satanic cults. The descriptions are eerily similar to the descriptions of the Order of the Nine Black Angels, which is located in Australia. Some satanic cults appear to be about control and torture of their victims starting in early childhood so that they can be used as sex slaves. There is a story about a young girl who committed suicide when

being forcibly returned to the cult after having run away.
The leader of this cult reportedly had been tortured in child-
hood as well.

Whether satanic cults exist or not, there are certainly
people who will use teenagers' fascination with the occult
to draw them into a vulnerable position where they can be
abused. Educating our young people about these dangers is
important.

A Biopsychosocial Theory of Violence

Epidemiological studies place the youth violence rate at about 30 percent for the last 20 years. There are no reliable estimates of the prevalence of child abuse in the U.S., although there are esti- mates that place the percentile of abused children between 7 and 40 percent. Several studies place the prevalence of mental health disorders in youths at 15 to 20 percent. The CARE study (Seifert, Phillips, and Parker 2001) attempted to examine the comorbidity among these conditions and suggested a model of a path for the development of youth violence.

The life of a violent young person is a matrix of complex interac- tive systems. Consequently, effective interventions will address the multiple subsystems in a holistic manner. Behavior can best be understood by examining the dynamics of the individual's biology and his/her social and physical context. The research literature indicates that there are six components of behavior:

1. Biological traits, genetic predisposition, and temperament

2. Family, attachment, bonding, and relationships

3. Individual characteristics including skills

4. Intelligence, education, and work

5. Development and learned behavior

6. Peer relationships

7. Cultural environment, shaping, and expectations

8. Protective factors and resiliency

Each dimension of a person's life can affect and be affected by another dimension. When the accumulation of negative factors and the absence of positive factors reaches a threshold, violence can occur.

1. Biological Traits, Genetic Predisposition, and Temperament

Violence may have a genetic or biological base in terms of temperament and volatility. Easygoing or irritable temperament can be seen from infancy. Those with a flexible, easygoing temperament seem to cope better with stress and are easier for parents to manage. There has been evidence that conduct disorders may have a genetic component.

Some genetically-based mental illnesses and psychiatric disorders such as schizophrenia will be expressed regardless of environmental insult. However, the severity may be related to the environmental and developmental context. Other illnesses require environmental or biological injury in order for the genetic predisposition to be expressed. For yet others, such as some forms of depression and anxiety, there may be no genetic element, but the environmental factors are so severe (such as child sexual abuse) that the illness develops.

Violent children often have a combination of symptoms, which can include hyperactivity, impulsivity, depression, anxiety, Obsessive/Compulsive and Bipolar symptoms, and psychosis. Another common factor is Attention Deficit Hyperactivity Disorder (ADHD), which is highly associated with delinquency and behavioral problems. "Children with both ADHD and verbal learning disabilities and/or social skill deficits present a more serious risk for sustaining their anti-social behavior through adolescence and into adulthood" (Fago 1999).

There are also certain brain development and neurological factors to consider. The environment provides the stimulus for the major shaping of the human brain for at least the first three or four years of life. Peak development is between ages 3 and 10, although the brain develops for a lifetime (The Secret Life of the Brain - *http://www.pbs.org/wnet/brain/index.html*). There is now research (Perry and Pollard 1997) to show that early trauma and neglect can change the function of the neurotransmitter system and brain size. Drs. Perry and Pollard (1997) found smaller brains among maltreated children when compared to non-maltreated children. This might explain the faulty perceiving and processing in this group. There are theories about the effect of neglect and trauma on the migration of brain cells in the first three years of life, and consequently the disrupted development of the frontal cortex, the limbic system, and higher cortical functions.

Dr. Pollack's work at the Baylor University Medical School found that maltreated children react to anger more strongly than non-abused children due to chronic elevation of stress and alarm neurotransmitters. Low IQ and deficient cognitive functioning can also be a factor. It can be a result of biology, traumatic events, or both, and it affects an individual's ability to cope. Recent studies have shown a relationship between immature brain development and enuresis (the uncontrolled or involuntary discharge of urine), a common characteristic of youth with DAP.

2. Family, Attachment, Bonding, and Relationships

Child abuse and neglect nearly doubled from 1.4 million in 1986 to 3 million in 1996. As many as 675,000 children annually are abused by their caregivers, who themselves may also be abusing alcohol and/or drugs. Of the 2,100 juvenile murder victims in 1997, 40 percent were killed by family members, 33 percent were under the age of 6, and 56 percent were killed with a firearm. A study by the Office of Juvenile Justice and Delinquency Prevention (OJJDP) showed that family members murdered 70 percent of younger juvenile murder victims, compared to 10 percent of older juvenile victims (September, 1999).

Approximately one in four girls and one in seven boys have been sexually abused. One third of all sexual assaults reported to authorities are against children younger than 12 (OJJDP September, 1999). Sexual abuse is a particularly devastating assault on a child. It causes children to withdraw and not trust others. These children also feel they are "bad and without redemption." They frequently do not blame abuse on the adult perpetrators; they blame themselves. *If I was only a better kid, this wouldn't be happening to me.* It can disrupt the bonding process and leave scars well into adulthood.

For many survivors of sexual abuse, pain, shame, and love become intertwined. Since everyone needs love, they may have difficulty separating love from pain. They are just as likely to be violent against themselves as others. Some portion of sexually abused children become violent perpetrators, while some engage in self-harming behaviors. Research has not yet identified which portion of the victimized population become abusers. It is an area in which further research is needed.

Dr. Cathy S. Widom studied a group of abused and neglected children from 1988 to 1996. She found significantly greater rates of general offending (49 percent) and violent offending (18 percent) among the group of abused and severely neglected children than the control group (38 percent had been arrested for any offense, 14 percent for a violent crime). She concluded that severe abuse and neglect are predictive of violent offending.

Violent children often come from families that are aggressive, violent, abusive, and neglectful. Family members are likely to have behavior problems, be weak in family bonding, show little warmth and nurturing, and have attitudes favorable to drug use and crime (Crespi and Rigazio-DiGilio 1996). Mothers with bonding issues from their own infancy, mental illness, sociopathy, or addiction problems may have difficulty nurturing and bonding with their infants. Children from homes with a single or teen parent, with poverty, and with large families are more likely to be abused or neglected. The teen birth rate in the U.S. is one of the highest (57 per 1,000 births) in the world. Rates in other industrialized nations range from 4 to 32 per 1,000 births (OJJDP September, 1999). The majority of at-tachment-disordered children that I have treated were raised in the first few years of life by mothers with addiction problems. Some have been adopted from foreign orphanages or foster care. When caregivers neglect or abuse their infants or expose them to domes-tic violence, problems with bonding ensue. Rage or apathy develops and is ever-present. This early interaction (or lack of) becomes the template for all future relationships.

This is not to say that single or teen parents are worse parents, just that their jobs are harder to begin with — and made harder still by a lack of programs and resources to help them. Likewise, most people who work in adoption and foster care agencies are good people doing the best they can for the children in their care, but are also lacking in the resources needed to properly nurture and develop every one of those children. It is also important to note that not all children, who are either raised by single or teen parents or adopted will grow up to be violent or have behavioral problems — far from it. This is just one of many factors, such as growing up in a violent neighborhood or lack of success in school, that can contribute to future behavioral problems. Many children who are exposed to these factors also have enough positive (resil-iency) factors in their lives to help them overcome the influence of violence. When parents — including single, teen, and adop-tive parents — create a loving, nurturing environment for their children, they can help them develop along a positive course and avoid violence.

We are familiar with "failure to thrive" babies who were raised in overcrowded Eastern European and turn-of-the-century American orphanages. These children were not held or nurtured and failed to mature and develop physically. Many died. Those who survived were unable to relate effectively to other people. The same process is at work with violent children who live in neglectful, abusive families and orphanages. When they are not nurtured or protected, they fail to thrive both emotionally and cognitively.

3. Individual Characteristics

Biology and environment can interact to create individual characteristics, such as being violent, that make a person vulnerable to ineffective coping. Violent children experience little emotion, but when they do, it can be explosive. Their ability to verbally and appropriately distinguish and communicate emotions is weak. They are unable to self-soothe or self-calm, something we learn as infants. If a nurturing parent is unavailable, the young child does not learn that skill. Violent children work themselves up until there's no turning back — it's a formula for disaster.

Lack of empathy may be exhibited in bullying, fights, and cruelty to animals. Exercising power over and being cruel to a helpless animal or smaller child can be an indicator of not having caring feelings about the welfare of other living beings. It can allow a child to harm or inflict pain on others without the pangs of conscience (Levy and Orlans 1999). These violent children's and teens' images of self are overwhelmingly negative; often they do not expect to succeed in our society by pro-social means. They are not successful in school, but they think they can be successful through antisocial means. Their reinforcement comes from antisocial peers.

Violent youth have often had early and persistent antisocial behavior, usually beginning with minor behavior problems at around age seven (OJJDP May 1998). This progresses to moderate problems at about age 9 and serious behavior problems around ages 11 or 12. They are often alienated, impulsive, and rebellious. Frequently, they have positive attitudes and beliefs about antisocial behaviors. They believe in the legitimacy of aggression as a means to an end. The deviant peer group often gives positive reinforcement for aggressive behavior and fills the need to be valued.

Violent individuals are often substance abusers and frequently come from substance-abusing families. They do not learn from their mistakes, nor are they able to delay gratification. They also have lower social anxiety than their pro-social peers. This has been demonstrated by the work of Dr. Hare. His book, *Without Conscience* (1993), is a good source of information. He determined that this difficulty in learning from mistakes is actually biological and has to do with arousal and fear responses.

4. Intelligence, Education, and Work

An intelligent child may be able to withstand the negative effects of a violent environment better than a child with less intelligence. He may be able to solve problems better and find resources for ameliorating difficulties. Intelligence can be a factor in the survival of an environmental injury. An intelligent child can be successful in school and thus receive necessary nurturing, self-esteem, and self-efficacy, even when it is not available at home. A less-intelligent child may not be successful in school and if he is not well-cared for at home or is abused, the lack of success at school compounds his negative self-image. Being bullied at school can also be a risk factor.

Many aggressive and violent children have borderline intellectual functioning and/or learning disabilities, and don't do well in school. Decline in cognitive functioning with increasing age has been observed among some violent teens. Chronically violent teens often have academic failure beginning in elementary school and consequently they lack a commitment to school. School offers no success or positive rewards for them.

5. Development and Learned Behavior

There are predictable sequences of child development. Children develop best in the shelter of a loving, nurturing environment, in which their needs are met. This gives them the safety to explore their surroundings. Caregivers can explain, assist, and teach. This helps the young of any species to proceed with regularity along a prescribed development path. Violence, abuse, trauma, neglect, and severe losses can interrupt and interfere with a child's normal developmental processes.

Caregivers who understand the child's point of view also help explain other people's perspectives so that a child can learn how to have empathy. They also provide a safe environment to explore and facilitate learning these skills. Violent children have not had this bonding experience, nor have they learned the necessary interpersonal skills to lead a successful life (Levy and Orlans 1998). They are still in an egocentric stage — the Me, Me, Me! stage. They lack empathy for others and do not expect others to cooperate with them. Consequently, these children have not learned the basic trust necessary for normal human relationships.

By age 11, children are learning to process abstract material and use logic to solve problems. If they have not had adults in their environment who answer "why" questions and explain the world to them, they may make mistakes in interpretation and they are less efficient in the problem-solving process. Logic is not fully developed for many children who perform violent acts. They often do not understand how to use cause and effect reasoning. This results in poor problem-solving skills. Eighty-eight percent of those with assault histories in the CARE study (r = .28) had problem-solving deficits. By contrast, 33 percent of those without behavior problem histories had difficulties with problem-solving.

Patterson, DeBaryshi, and Ramsey (1989) described a sequence of social learning events that lead to a sustained delinquency, and hence violence. The pre-delinquent uses aversive behaviors to get what she wants from other family members. They, in turn, attempt to coerce the child into submission. The coercive behaviors escalate on both sides. When the child gets her way in this manner, her aversive behaviors are reinforced. Eighty-two percent of those in the CARE study with assaultive histories (r = .30) had delayed social development. Thirty percent of those without behavior problems had poor social skills.

Violence can be a learned coping style. Children observe the people and events around them. They believe that the behavior of the adults around them exemplify optimal adult behavior. They practice what they see in an effort to develop what they believe to be acceptable behavior. If you watch preschool children, you will see that they play with dress-up clothing, dolls, and action figures. They are practicing what it is to be an adult.

If the adults in their lives solve problems in a violent manner, that becomes the norm for expected behavior. Statistically, we know that 79 percent of violent children have witnessed violence between their parents, and that violent children are four times more likely to come from homes with parental violence. Neighborhood and community violence and war are also factors. Children repeat what they see.

Additionally, there are natural reinforcers within the family structure for certain behaviors. Young children, because of their developmental stage, are egocentric and need immediate gratification. They will do whatever it takes to get their needs met. If whining gets them what they want, then whining becomes a pattern that is reinforced and hard to break as long as the child gets what she wants from it. Behavior can be aggressive as well. If hitting gets a child what she wants, then it will become a pattern. Likewise, if she doesn't get nurturing at home but does get it from a peer group, then she will seek out nurturing from the group and become very attached to it. She will repeat behaviors reinforced by the group.

For examples of this we might look to the work of Konrad Lorenz, who in 1935 described the learning behavior of young ducklings and goslings as a process of imprinting. Soon after the critical stage of hatching, the young will emulate a parent or surrogate's visual and auditory actions, such as quacking. (Lorenz became a "mother figure" for a group of ducklings.)

Just as there are stages of physical and emotional development, there is a progression of moral development throughout one's lifetime. In 1969, Kohlberg studied the moral development of boys. He wrote stories of ethical dilemmas and then studied how boys of different ages viewed the scenarios. His stages of Moral Development are found in Chapter 3.

6. Peer Relationships

Success and positive self-worth are universal needs. When children fail to fulfill them, they look for other youths with similar problems and views. In this deviant peer culture, they can become successful in their own eyes and the eyes of peers. In taking the peer group away from them, a new route to success must be forged. These children find it difficult to relate to "straight" kids. They think, feel, and act differently, and straight kids are the peers that previously rejected them. Closing that gap can be a considerable task. Another indicator of future risk may be a pattern of fighting with and bullying other students.

Pro-social peer group rejection and school failure alienate and separate these youths from conventional activities, socialization processes, and attachment to the larger community outside their homes, such as those found in churches, schools, and organized sports. This, then, becomes a significant precursor to either social withdrawal or joining a deviant peer group. The deviant peer group or the immersion in a nihilistic subculture or ideology gives the youth structure, identity, and a sense of belonging. Violent behaviors can be praised and reinforced by these antisocial subcultures. We have seen examples in groups of teens such as the Trench Coat Mafia, who carried out the Columbine attacks, MS-13, a very violent and rapidly growing gang now in 33 states, and similar violence-driven groups.

Some risk factors of gang membership (Howell, 1998):

- High crime neighborhood
- Availability of drugs and firearms
- Lack of economic opportunities
- Substance abuse by families
- Family violence
- Family gang membership
- Lack of school success
- Delinquent peer group
- History of delinquency
- Excitement-seeking
- Selling drugs
- Childhood trauma

7. Cultural Enviornment, Shaping, and Expectations

Overall, teenagers are at a greater risk for being victims of violence
than adults of any age (Bureau of Justice Statistics data on victims
of violent crimes 2004). Victims of violence who are not protected or
provided treatment and a safe environment in which to heal are at
risk of becoming violent. If the community is one where there exists
both an easy availability of and community standards that favor the
use of drugs and firearms, and if there is an acceptance of crime as a
way of life, the children of that neighborhood are more likely to use
violent means to accomplish their goals.

According to Dr. Deborah Prothrow-Stith (1993), by the time most
children in developed countries are grown, they have seen 100,000
acts of violence on television, video games, and film. Many experts
agree that media violence negatively affects children. A child who,

daily or weekly, shoots and batters people on a video game can become hardened to the harm that an aggressive acts in reality do to another. Youths with DAP may be more vulnerable to the influence of media violence.

If you live in America, it's likely you believe in The American Dream. Commercials encourage the desire for the tangible signs of prosperity. When extreme economic deprivation, poor school performance, and other factors cause the path of pro-social success to be blocked or unavailable, teens may seek out other, often antisocial, means to have money, "things", and power.

Additionally, in our modern Western culture, male children are undergoing a miseducation. They are often taught that being a real man means being stoic and macho. The only emotion they are encouraged to express is anger. The expression of softer emotions, such as crying, are taboo for many men. They are encouraged to not be "sissies." Schools continue to favor sedentary rather than active learning. This places boys who are naturally active at a disadvantage (Murray 1999).

In addition to ingrained gender learning differences, boys have the media sending them distorted messages. The mainstream media glorifies the mindless killing machine. In the last few decades, society has successfully challenged feminine stereotypes, but it has yet to do so in the images and characters that allow boys to think and feel outside the norm. Men who want to offer boys another type of role model may feel constrained by the cultural pressure to conform to the stereotype. This is no different than the challenging of the female stereotype that began in the 1960's. However, the outcome may be different. "When we don't let boys cry tears, some will cry bullets," is one popular quote that I feel rings true (W. Pollack and Murray 1999).

We know that cultures and subcultures differ in their customs and expectations of behavior. If a child grows up in an environment where there are significant amounts of violence in the neighborhood, this will become a behavioral expectation. While not all children succumb to this expectation, it affects everyone in some way. Some have the strength, support, and skills to resist the pull, and others do not. It is a combination of risk and resiliency factors that reflect how the various influences over a child will be expressed.

8. Protective Factors & Resiliency

Travis Hirschi's 1969 social learning theory has been an important theory for understanding youth violence. According to Hirschi, non-delinquents have social bonds that contain four elements:

1. Attachment to parents, peers, and school.

2. Commitment to conventional lines of action (e.g., deferred gratification, work ethic, the value of education).

3. Involvement in conventional activities (e.g., school, sports, family activities, work).

4. Belief in the moral order (e.g., traditional ideas of right and wrong; the idea that right will prevail and wrong will fail).

These four factors form the basis of resiliency. They give us hints as to where to proceed with interventions.

Many youths with DAP do not have these traits. They often lack constant, positive, and nurturing caregivers who set rules, respect a child's individuality, and provide secure attachment in order for them to grow up to be emotionally healthy. School success and having pro-social peers can be a protective factor. Having a positive social orientation is also helpful. Higher IQ and resilient temperament can help a child heal from environmental insults and learn to cope more effectively. When there are bonds to supportive pro-social family, teachers, counselors, or other adults, kids have a chance to make choices other than resorting to violence. Clearly stated family and community rules and expectations as well as monitoring of behavior can be effective in helping children learn to follow social norms. A child who has good social and problem-solving skills, moral maturity, and an ability to manage emotions, particularly handling anger effectively, will have fewer problems with violence. Children who are curious and enthusiastic, set goals for themselves, have high self-esteem, and have an internal locus of control will be more resilient (Levy and Orlans 1998).

The Additive Nature of Risk and Resiliency Factors

The Office of Juvenile Justice and Delinquency Prevention (OJJDP) has identified risk and protective factors for youth violence. According to OJJDP, children with more than five risk factors and less than six protective factors have an 80 percent chance of committing future violent acts (Howell, May 1995).

Risk Factors (More than 5):
- Lack of healthy guidance and monitoring from care givers

- Lack of academic success
- Learning problems
- Psychological problems
- Attending disorganized and disruptive schools
- Inability to be successful among pro-social peers
- Living in chaotic neighborhoods
- Access to few resources for positive activities
- Maltreatment
- Living in a community high in drug use, guns, violence, gangs and delinquency

Protective Factors (Less than 6):
- Resilient temperament
- Close relationship with pro-social, supportive adult
- Clear standards of behavior set by care givers
- Adults who provide encouragement
- Adults who provide healthy beliefs
- Skills that help them be successful in school or other activities
- Opportunities to be successful

The most salient risk factors, according to various studies, appear to be:
- Violent family background
- Attachment disorder
- Cruelty to animals
- Prior assault, especially if on an authority figure
- Fire-setting
- Enuresis and encopresis
- Escape from secure custody of an agency

(For more on behavior as a function see Diagram 1.)

In the following chapter, I will show how violence is affecting children all over the world. Why, you ask, should you in your comfortable recliner at home in America care? International youth violence has an undeniably strong connection to terrorism. Terrorism has thrashed its deadly claws many times on our own soil, most memorably in the September 11 attacks, and it is threat that molds much U.S. foreign and domestic policy.

Chapter 5

The Problem of Violence in Every Corner of the World

The earliest historical records and archeological evidence dating back thousands of years tell us that humankind has repeatedly seen mass suffering at the onset of wars, plagues, and natural disasters. Chaos, death, cruelty, and fear belong to every era, albeit in different forms. My parents' generation had Hitler, Nazism, and fascism; it was a time when the world's balance of power was shifting and new military technology, such as nuclear energy and the atom bomb, became a horrifying threat to civilization.

A new, unprecedented violence is burgeoning in our modern era. Terrorism is redefining the rules of warfare. At the dawn of the new millennium, we saw the largest foreign attack on domestic soil in the events of September 11, 2001. The U.S. and its allies took swift action against Osama bin Laden in Afghanistan in response to these attacks. However, with the rising death toll on both sides in the war in Iraq — despite the lack of connection between Saddam Hussein and 9/11 — doubt has been cast on the intentions of the United States in the eyes of the international community. Yet in the pictures of the Abu Ghraib prison abuse scandal, many recognize that the perpetuance of violence can be in the name of authority.

We used to think that violence took place only in city streets and countries at war. Now it manifests in churches, schools, rural areas, and small towns. We saw it in the school shootings in Erfurt, Germany where an expelled 19-year-old killed 14 staff members, two students, a police officer, and himself in 2002, and in the massacre at the elementary school in Beslan, Russia in 2004. Kids kill kids and kids rape other kids. Violence in the United States and all over the world claims millions of victims yearly; the AIDS pandemic, the underground sex trade, ethnic cleansing, and genocide keep people living in a constant state of fear, pain, and degradation. Rape, domestic violence, assault, and greed are rampant in our neighborhoods and abroad. No nation has been spared. Disrupted attachment may be the source of many of these forms of violence.

The World's Street Children: Surviving War, Poverty, AIDS, and Terrorism

In my travels to countries around the world I've witnessed countless children living on the street, begging for food and money. In several of these countries, such as China, the Philippines, Brazil, and, to a lesser extent, Peru, the rampant, visible poverty startled my consciousness and touched my heart. In the rest of this chapter, I use my own experiences to illustrate how vital it is that the world's children not be forgotten.

The Philippines
Half of the world's population lives in the Asia-Pacific region. Thirty

percent of this population lives in poverty, and 40 percent of the total population is children. The number of street children is unknown because they are not counted. It is estimated that there are millions of street children in this region of the world. Many are controlled by criminal gangs, most have been abused and all have been neglected (West 2003).

The Philippines is a beautiful country populated with warm, resourceful, friendly people; it is rich in both natural resources and extreme poverty. If you talk to some of the locals, they will say that they believe that their tax money pays for the excesses of corrupt politicians rather than the needs of the people. There is a great problem with abandoned street-dwelling children begging for food and money here. It is estimated that there are 1.5 million desperate street kids in this country (West 2003). I even encountered a few children living on the street that went without clothing.

In parts of Cebu, where Americans are warned to not go out at night, my husband Rick and I saw a 5- or 6-year-old girl carrying what appeared to be a one-year-old child on her hip. It was something I could have never emotionally prepared myself to see. Thirty percent of street children in the Philippines are female, and many of them are exploited and sexually abused, their bodies sold as a commodity into the sex trade. In this and many other parts of the world, there are agencies that provide sex tourism.

Foreigners seeking sex with minors can visit a brothel in almost any country of the world and have sex with a partner of any age or gender of their choosing. Brothels and child pornography abound and profits are in the millions, if not billions. Parents living in poverty, or who prefer to have sons, will sell girls into brothels. Some of these children go willingly with anyone who will promise them food, protection, and a place to live. Most have no idea what awaits.

If you have seen the movies *Memoirs of a Geisha* (2005) and *Born into Brothels* (2004), you have seen one fictional and one real account (respectively) of how this process works. Brothels and pornography studios are not just in far away lands that you have never heard of, they are right here in the U.S.; the sex trade goes on daily in all large cities spanning the globe.

Some girls are used as "drug mules" (a good film for background on drug mules is *Maria Full of Grace* [2004]). Drug mules swallow large quantities of drugs wrapped in bags and are sent on airplanes into the U.S. or other countries to deliver the contraband. Their payment is a trip out of poverty and into another nation. If the bags break, the drug mule dies from an overdose, but the supply of willing men and women is endless. I can't help but think that certain members of the human race have lost their moral compass, and some of us have our heads in the sand.

Neglected male children, on the other hand, are often used in theft rings and drug trafficking. Authorities often place these young people living on the streets in adult prisons for long periods of time for minor offenses — you can imagine what damage having prison inmates as role models would do to a child. In or out of prison, by the time they grow up, they will likely be bitter and antisocial. Their attachment patterns will be disrupted, and committing acts of violence will become as natural as playing cowboys and robbers is for boys growing up in America. It is my impression that these street kids will do anything for survival. Because of such desperate conditions, these young, vulnerable boys are ripe pickings for terrorist organizations.

Al-Qaeda operates a terrorist recruitment and training camp on the Philippines' second-largest island, Mindanao. In May 2004, the acting United States ambassador to the Philippines, Joseph Mussomeli, described Mindanao as the world's new terrorist "Mecca" in comparison to Afghanistan. "Certain portions of Mindanao are so lawless, so porous...that you run the risk of it becoming like an Afghanistan situation," he said on the news program *Dateline*. He said there exist alliances between Mindanao Muslim insurgency groups and Al Qaeda, as well as the Indonesian-based terrorist group Jemaah Islamiyah.

During our trip to the Philippines, there were reports of searches on Mindanao for two terrorists; the million dollar U.S. bounty was equal to a small fortune there. Americans were told to be extremely careful because it was feared that terrorists would kidnap them for use as bargaining chips. Although we were not on Mindanao, we were an hour away by boat, staying in a hotel frequented by Americans and Canadians.

One morning at breakfast, an angry-looking young man with piercing black eyes, olive skin, and shiny, black hair surreptitiously watched us eat our breakfast on our hotel patio. He was impeccably dressed, reading a newspaper, and not eating. He whispered something on his cell phone and continued to watch us from behind his paper. Meanwhile, we too were reading the newspaper: headlines of "Caution to Americans" gave us goose bumps. As you can imagine, that was one of the scariest mornings of my life. Whether the threat this mysterious man posed was real or imagined, we weren't going to waste time finding out. Post haste, we left the restaurant and the Philippines. Young street boys are ideal targets for terrorist organizations; with their lack of education, limited or non-existent capacity for empathy, and detestation for authority, these boys are willing candidates. After all, what has society ever done for *them*? Their impressionable minds easily absorb religious fundamentalist propaganda — a cause that offers acceptance, camaraderie, and a support system never before afforded them (however brutal and hateful it may be). While it's virtually impossible for us in Western societies to fathom a human being strapping explosives to his body to inflict maximum pain and suffering on others, what does the boy underneath have to lose? The promise of spiritual fulfillment is infinitely more motivating than a meager existence of victimization on the streets.

I believe that if we want to stop terrorism, we must find a way to take care of the abandoned street children around the world and eliminate this terrorist recruitment base.

China

Despite the establishment of protection centers for street children in China, it is estimated that in this country of 1.3 billion citizens, there are 200,000 children living on the streets. This does not include children who have families and must work for survival (West 2003).

In China, my husband and I saw groups of street children begging in crowded markets. The ill-clothed children appeared to be as young as three or four. They had taken plastic milk cartons, cut out the bottoms, turned them upside down, and were using them as money containers for begging. There were hoards of begging children everywhere we went. Our guide told us not to give them money because word would spread and we would be mobbed by children for the rest of the trip. We didn't give them money, but it was very difficult not to.

South Africa

There are 5.6 million people living with HIV in South Africa, and almost 1,000 people die of AIDS every day, according to the Department for International Development. Around 1,500 people become infected with HIV daily. The Centre for Actuarial Research at the University of Cape Town estimates there are currently about 3.4 million children under the age of 18 in South Africa who have lost one or both parents to the disease, called AIDS orphans. By 2015, statisticians predict there will be 4.6 million AIDS orphans in the country.

When I visited South Africa, I didn't see as many children out on the street as I had expected from reading such startling statistics. In this country where a high adult mortality rate offers a life expectancy of 47 years, I imagined the outcome to be an overwhelming prevalence of displaced and orphaned children. Indeed, they do exist. Yet on my trip I didn't see many of them. In South Africa, I learned, it is common for relatives to take in children who have lost their parents.

My husband and I visited South Africa's townships of Khayelitsha and Soweto in 2000. Few cars drove along the dirt roads here; instead, they were dotted with sleeping dogs and crowded with meandering people. The houses and small stores seemed to have been pieced together with scraps of wood and cardboard and topped with perforated tin roofs. Many homes consisted of one-room dirt floors with plastic chairs similar to the ones you can buy for $5 in the U.S. and that last forever. Hand-painted signs designated the local mom-and-pop stores. The areas were clean, with very little rubbish lying about. Neighborhood residents utilized an outdoor hand pump at a well for drinking water, carrying full buckets back to their homesteads.

The people who were born and raised in these townships seemed to love their neighborhoods as much as you and I love ours. Even when they earned enough money to move out of the township, those I spoke with said they chose to stay and help build better houses for others in the area. They were extraordinarily hopeful, resilient people. They welcomed us warmly. Many had set up souvenir shops or spread blankets on the ground to display their hand-made art and jewelry for sale.

We saw many families, especially grandparents, who had taken in orphaned children. Even in the poorer townships, the camaraderie in caring for children is evident. Miss Vicky, who owns a bed and breakfast in Khayelitsha Township is one example. The money she earned at her B&B was used to help take care of community children.

Miss Vicky was a warm, pleasant woman who laughed easily. Her plump figure and round features were accented by her traditional African dress and a scarf with a bright green floral pattern. While Miss Vicky's looked like any other modest township home from the outside, the inside was quite large, had individual rooms, and had been decorated quite nicely in traditional African décor. It had wooden floors. I don't know about the plumbing situation — it was not something about which I wished to inquire — although I'm sure it was rudimentary at best.

Miss Vicky has taken in six orphaned children from the neighborhood. To help raise money for the children, on a table she keeps an institutional-size plastic mayonnaise jar to accept cash donations. On the jar is a picture of local children and a single statement, which reads, "Please help the children of Khayelitsha Township." Miss Vicky doesn't beg or push for donations, like others I have seen in different countries, but goes about the process with a sort of nonchalant tact. On the mayonnaise jar's notice, she mentions that the money will be used to take the children of the township on field trips or to help them get uniforms so they can attend school. Miss Vicky is an anomaly and, while I wish she didn't have to ask for money for her children, I support her non-intrusive way of doing so. Miss Vicky's was a highlight of one of the best trips I've ever had, and I highly recommend visiting if you have the opportunity. Because Miss Vicky has a web page, people come from all over the world to stay in her bed and breakfast and experience the township life.

Apartheid may have been abolished in South Africa, and yet the gap between the "haves" and the "have-nots" is still great. Beyond the poor yet hopeful townships I visited, it is common for those with money to live in houses behind stone walls with broken glass embedded in the tops to keep robbers out. South Africa's future will depend on how its government and the international community can care for its numerous poor and ill. Abandoned children, even if adopted into extended families, will face similar fates to their parents if they are not educated about the ways in which HIV and AIDS are spread and the proper prevention methods — and given access to affordable methods of preventing the spread of the disease.

Peru

My husband and I saw many children peddling goods with their families on the streets in Peru. Relatively speaking, we saw fewer abandoned children in Peru than we did in other countries. We noted that if the family was poor, each family member, however old, was out on the streets with his or her hand open. This is what we saw in Cusco. In a country of 29 million, it is estimated that there are over one million children making their living in the Peruvian streets for survival.

There are several non-profit and charity organizations that have established shelters and education centers for Peruvian street children, such as Street Kids Peru (*http://streetkidsperu.com*). Those who volunteer for such organizations report that a major problem is Peruvian parents rejecting their children when they cannot take care of them. Often boys are thrown out of their homes at the age of 4 or 5 and forced to fend for themselves. Volunteers say these boys' life expectancies are very low; they often die by age 12, sometimes of hypothermia in the chilling night temperatures. Many organizations have achieved relative success in bringing children out of the streets and into classrooms.

Brazil

I experienced first-hand the aggressiveness of Brazil's street children on a trip to Rio De Janeiro. While I didn't see any children begging on the streets like I did in the Philippines, China, and Peru, when my husband and I were shopping in this bustling metropolis, I saw the ease at which teens resort to violence for survival. My husband and I were aggressively mugged by four teenagers and young adults.

We arrived in Rio De Janeiro around mid-morning in the middle of summer. Our rooms weren't ready, so we decided to explore a bit of town before our travel guide's orientation lecture. This soon proved to be a mistake. We wandered into an area on the edge of the hotel zone where street vendors were selling t-shirts, knick knacks, and local art and jewelry.

We entered a corner where a mother and young child were selling their wares. The mother had a card table and was sitting in a metal kitchen chair feeding rice to her toddler in her lap. We were perusing t-shirts when we were suddenly surrounded by four teenagers and young adults in swim trunks, their lean, muscular chests exposed. They were members of one of Rio De Janeiro's many roving mini-gangs of extremely hostile teens who spread terror on the streets to get what they need (watch the movie *City of God* for a first-rate portrayal [2003]).

The young men were very strong and fit; we were middle-aged Americans. Rick, bless his heart, was in good shape. He attended the gym regularly, practiced martial arts, and lifted weights. Although I have martial arts training as well, I was out of shape and at a disadvantage. While one whipped out a very large two-fisted screwdriver, two more held my husband's arms firmly on each side. The one with the screwdriver started to poke Rick's chest with the makeshift weapon, and the fourth tore at his trouser pockets. They tore his pants down the seam from top to bottom, but Rick diligently held onto the opening in his pocket where his money was. He yelled to me to run.

Run I did, and of course I still had the t-shirts in my hand, so the lady from the booth started running after me because she thought I was stealing them. I saw her, dropped the t-shirts, and ran for my life, not knowing if my husband would escape or not. I knew I couldn't help him, and I was comforted in the knowledge that he was strong. He wrestled free from the young men and ran after me across a wide-open field and back to the hotel.

We got away with our lives and our money. The story of our "adventure" and "Rick's physical prowess" became lore among the others in the tour group as our trip continued. At the orientation, we were told not to take any money, jewelry, or cameras on the street or to the beach — tidbits of information that would have come in handy moments earlier. When Rick tells the story now, he says, "There was sweat from hard work on every one of those dollar bills, and I wasn't about to give them up without a fight."

Our four teenager aggressors likely had attachment problems due to early maltreatment and neglect. Those boys had learned to survive, not by trusting adults but by taking what they wanted and using force (early childhood stage of moral development). It was ironic for my husband and I to be at the receiving end of such brutality, after I've studied the causes of violence for decades. However, understanding violence made me no less afraid when that boy with the screwdriver was threatening to harm the person most dear to me. My husband and I were in the wrong place at the wrong time; our travel savvy has increased exponentially since.

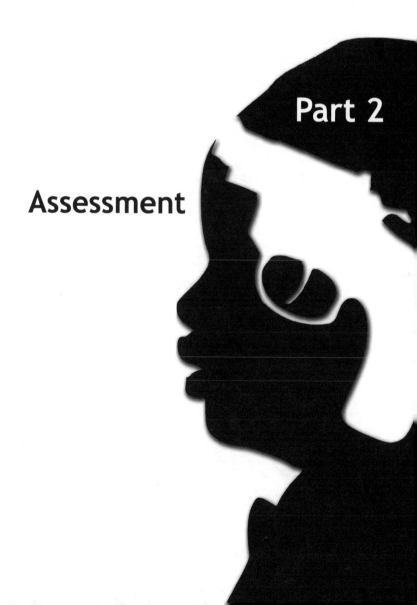

Part 2

Assessment

Chapter 6

Assessment for Disrupted Attachment Patterns (DAP)

There are varying combinations of ADHD, Oppositional Defiant Disorder (ODD), and Conduct Disorder (CD) in traditional diagnoses of those with severe behavioral and interpersonal problems. For adults with severe personality disorders, behavioral problems, and unstable interpersonal relationships, men tend to be diagnosed with antisocial personality disorder and women borderline personality disorder or Dissociative Identity Disorder — yet the relationship among these disorders needs to be clarified by further research.

These diagnoses may fall on a continuum from very appropriate behavioral and interpersonal behaviors (altruistic), to average levels of appropriate behaviors (pro-social), to severely inappropriate behaviors (psychopathy/attachment disorders). On one end of the continuum there is Mother Theresa and Gandhi, most of the population falls somewhere in the middle, people with personality disorders are at the three-quarters mark, and psychopaths and severely attachment-disordered children are at the far end of the continuum.

Figure 6. A Theoretical Continuum of Interpersonal Dimensions

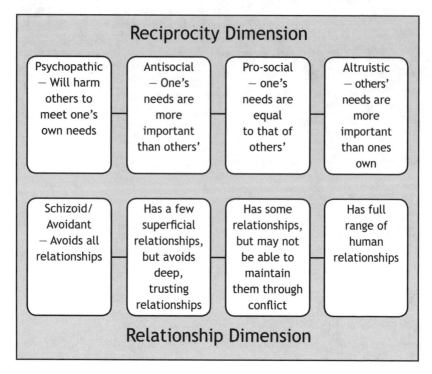

Looking at the continuum above, the logical question is: How do people come to be where they are on the spectrum? Each person's unique combination of risk and resiliency factors ultimately results in a person's placement on the continuum (above). People can move along the continuum according to circumstances and the ability of the adults in the child's life to support healthy relationship skill development.

A Model of the Development of Violent and Other Inappropriate Social Behaviors

The development and quality of interpersonal skills depends on:

- Physical Environment
- Social Environment
- A Person's Physiology
- A Person's Psychological/Developmental Make

Any and all of the factors in the above charts can affect the youth's developmental trajectory. Measuring the symptoms of an attachment problem is the beginning of the process of determining the youth's level of skills and how to support healthy development.

Measuring Attachment across the Life Cycle

Bowlby proposed that internal self-other working models, constructed in the context of early childhood attachment relationships, are foundational for personality development. A preponderance of research exists that supports this theoretical proposition. Evidence suggests that the security of early childhood attachment relates to a number of childhood psychosocial problems. Such problems include psychological disorders, violent and antisocial behavior, and tendencies to associate with deviant peer groups.

While security of attachment seems to have profound implications for later life psychosocial functioning, traditional methods for assessing attachment styles are lengthy, time-consuming, and expensive to implement. These procedures severely limit the number of subjects that can be studied at one time. Additionally, such studies are generally amenable only to those professionals trained in either the direct observation procedure (i.e., Strange Situation) or the clinical interview (i.e., Adult Attachment Interview).

The Attachment Disorder Assessment Scale for Children

An important standard of social work practice in the 21st century is the continued need for empirically validated and competent assessment tools for working with clients. Children with attachment disorders are an area in mental health practice that needs expansion of standardized measurements in order to make appropriate assessments. Among children receiving social services, research shows a continual rise in the number of children with severe attachment disorder. However, I will outline a few helpful resources whose contact information I have placed in a side bar on page 96.

The Attachment Disorder Assessment Scale

The Attachment Disorder Assessment Scale (ADAS) is a newly-designed, multidimensional assessment designed to measure attachment disorder in children ranging in age from 1 to 13 years. It is administered to primary full-time caregivers of children. These include biological, adoptive, and foster care parents, as well as grandparents and other kinship caregivers. For inclusion in the study, each primary caregiver fulfilled the role of a custodial supervisor of a child for at least one month. From June 1999 to May 2000, 449 primary caregivers completed the ADAS.

The ADAS is a 40-item self-report instrument scored on a three-point Likert scale. Items were formulated from attachment theory concepts and the DSM-IV criteria for Reactive Attachment Disorder. Reliability analysis indicated a high degree of internal consistency (alpha = .94). Validity analyses indicated evidence of construct validity. The ADAS correlates highly with a mental health diagnosis of attachment disorder and discriminates between a diagnosis of attachment disorder/reactive attachment disorder and attention deficient hyperactivity disorder. Limitations of the study, implications for social work practice, and future research are discussed.

Security of Adult Attachment and the Relationship between Intimate Partner Violence and Substance Abuse

According to attachment theory, childhood attachment experiences help the infant to form internal working models (schema) of self and of others. These internal working models are foundational to personality development and guide all subsequent interpersonal behavior. Several measures of adult attachment are now utilized in research investigating various adult social behaviors. Intimate partner violence is one such area of research. Recent studies indicate that security of attachment relates to a propensity for partner violence. Though few, if any, studies exist that propose a relationship between security of adult attachment and substance abuse, such a proposition makes theoretical sense.

This study proposes that security of attachment not only relates to a propensity for intimate-partner violence, but to a propensity for substance abuse as well. To test this proposition, a sample of 100 men from a substance abuse facility, 100 men from a spousal abuse treatment facility, and 100 men from the general population are compared. In a cross-sectional format, subjects complete a variety of measures, including the Relationship Scales Questionnaire. The Relationship Scales Questionnaire is based on the self-other dimensions of attachment and can be used to classify subjects into secure, dismissing, preoccupied, and fearful prototypes.

Research hypotheses predict that those classified into fearful and preoccupied attachment prototypes will be more likely to use violent behavior than those classified as either secure or dismissing. Theoretically, if internal self-other working models formed during early childhood attachment experiences relate to security of adult self-other working models, and if insecure self-other working models relate to intimate partner abuse and substance abuse, then interventions that enhance the quality of the infant caretaker relationship should help reduce both intimate partner violence and substance abuse.

The Assessment of Children with Attachment Disorder: The Randolph Attachment Disorder Questionnaire, The Behavioral and Emotional Rating Scale, and The Biopsychosocial Attachment Types Framework

Children with attachment disorder (AD) have an ongoing risk of mental health challenges and an exacerbated resistance to traditional treatments (Dozier, Stovall, and Albus 1999). The inability to trust and inadequate relationship skills present a substantial challenge for supervising adults in families, child welfare, juvenile justice, public schools, and other community settings (Solomon and George 1999).

This study examined the assessment of AD in children between ages 6 and 18 utilizing two standardized instruments, the Randolph Attachment Disorder Questionnaire (RADQ, Randolph 1997) and the Behavioral and Emotional Rating Scale (BERS, Epstein and Sharma 1998). A framework developed by the author, Biopsychosocial Attachment Types (BAT), for conceptualizing childhood attachment concerns, was explored as a foundation for assessment and as a guide for an incremental corrective experiential approach for altering the child's internal working model of attachment. Biophilia and attachment theories were explanatory for the BAT (Bowlby 1988; Kellert 1997).

Three research questions were explored. First, can scores on the BERS be used to predict attachment disorder as measured by the RADQ? Second, can the categories of the BAT be measured using selected BERS items plus additional author-developed items? Finally, if selected BERS additional items are found to measure the BAT categories, then are the resulting measures reliable and valid? The Foster Family Survey questionnaire, completed by 285 foster parents of children 6 to 18 years old who had been in care for over three months in British Columbia, Canada, provided the data collected in 1999.

Reported results included an 18-item BAT measure and a 7-item subscale that predicted RADQ scores. The regression equation for the RADQ score predicted from the BAT yielded a cumulative adjusted $r2$ of .515. The resulting BAT measure achieved an alpha score of .91 and factor analysis distinguished the categories. All of these results supported the continued value of research in this area of investigation (Marvin and Britner 1999).

Resource Contact Information

The Attachment Disorder Assessment Scale for Children
Sherry Fairchild-Kienlen, MSSW, Ph.D. Student
University of Texas at Arlington
3804 Whiffletree Court
Plano, Texas 75023
Email: sfair@flash.net

Security of Adult Attachment and the Relationship Between
Intimate Partner Violence and Substance Abuse
Alan J. Lipps, LMSW, Ph.D. Student
University of Texas at Arlington
5819 Sandhurst Lane, Apt. D.
Dallas, Texas 75206

The Assessment of Children with Attachment Disorder: The
Randolph Attachment Disorder Questionnaire, The Behavioral
and Emotional Rating Scale, and The Biopsychosocial Attach-
ment Types Framework
A. Myrth Ogilvie, Ph.D., M.S.W.
Assistant Professor of Social Work
University of Washington, Tacoma Box 358425,
1900 Commerce Street
WCG 203
Tacoma, WA 98402-3100

Information found on the internet at *http://www.sswr.org/*
papers2001/420.htm; The Society for Social Work Research.
Author Unknown.

The RADQ, by Dr. Liz Randolph, has been one of the most widely used instruments to measure childhood attachment disorders. Information about it can be found at *http://www.instituteforattachment.org/entry/results.php?article_id=41*. Appropriate ages for this tool are from 5 to 18 years of age. Dr. Randolph suggests that her tool can distinguish between attachment disorders and other childhood behavior problems. There are three subscales for this tool: anxious, avoidant, and ambivalent types of attachment disorders. There have been both supporters and critics of the RADQ and Dr. Randolph (2000). Critiques can be found at the following websites:

http://www.srmhp.org/0102/attachment-therapy.html

http://www.medscape.com/viewarticle/508956_3

The primary criticisms have been about the lack of research in the attachment field in general and specifically this instrument. Supporters say that this is a new area of inquiry and it will take time to build a body of literature. In the interim, we need to pursue research at every level.

CARE Attachment Subscale

For help in interpreting the CARE, which I completed in 2003, and to add to its utility, there are now four subscales: Chronic Violence, Sexual Behavior Problems, Attachment Problems, and Psychiatric Problems. These subscales are adjuncts to the original CARE, which contains the Case Management Planning Form and guides intervention planning.

The Attachment Subscale of the CARE (Seifert 2006) is a newly created instrument for assessing problems that are less well-known than violence or sexual behavior problems, but may be at the root of the more overt inappropriate social behaviors. Knowing when a child has disrupted attachment problems or trauma issues can guide treatment and, hopefully, prevent future violence and sexual offending. As the other subscales, it is intended to be used with the original CARE to take advantage of the treatment planning aspects of that tool.

The sample includes 823 youths. Items on this subscale are severely deficient problem-solving skills, history of attachment symptoms, bullying, early abuse and neglect, exposure to domestic violence, school difficulties, caregivers who have untreated psychiatric or substance abuse problems, and parental abandonment. Participation in a positive, pro-social activity is a protective factor. Statistical analysis was used to provide psychometric properties of the subscale.

- Eta = .72; Eta2 = .51; p = .00, ROC = .90 (with clinically assessed attachment problems)
- 59 percent (499) with no attachment issues
- 27 percent (224) with mild to moderate attachment/Family Trauma Problems
- 14 percent (119) with severe Attachment (disorganized/dismissive) Disorder

Those with mild to moderate scores may need family trauma therapy, while those with the highest scores will need trauma and attachment work as well as skill-building.

This subscale of the CARE identifies youths who may have attachment difficulties. The CARE case management tool provides a structure to develop a plan for intervention for a youth having behavioral problems. In addition to this, an assessment of where the youth is in the developmental sequence in interpersonal, self-regulation, and other skill areas will be useful. The Behavioral Objective Sequence by Dr. Sheldon Braaten is just such a tool.

Behavioral Objective Sequence

Accurate assessment of behavioral skills is essential in developing effective intervention programs for students with emotional and behavioral disorders (EBD). Assessment is the foundation for determining individually relevant intervention goals, objectives, and plans, as well as for monitoring intervention outcomes. Several criteria for effective assessment have been identified in the literature. Among them are use of multiple sources (i.e., teachers and other professionals, parents, and students themselves) as well as use of culturally appropriate types of measurement instruments (intellectual, achievement, and behavioral) and procedures (observations and interviews). Behavioral assessment traditionally focuses on identifying problem behaviors; however, it is important to determine students' existing strengths upon which new pro-social skills can be built. Few instruments focus upon student strengths.

Recently there has been an increasing emphasis on strength-based or competency-based assessment (Epstein 1999). Some benefits of competency-based assessments are that they (a) yield information that can actually be used for individualized education program (IEP) planning, (b) provide a positive view of the student by specifying student strengths, and (c) delineate pro-social behaviors not yet mastered that require instruction and differential reinforcement. Epstein's Behavioral and Emotional Rating Scale (BERS), Gresham and Elliott's Social Skills Rating System (SSRS), and the Walker-McConnell Scale are examples of other strength-based rating scales. DuPaul and Eckerts's (1994) review of seven studies of social skills training programs found that efficacious curricula emphasize student competencies as opposed to performance deficits.

Behavioral assessment instruments should present pro-social skills within an appropriate developmental sequence. Youth will have behavioral difficulties and skills that vary according to their progression through the developmental levels (Vernon 1993). A delicate task of assessment is to distinguish between problems of children and youth that are considered "normal" at various developmental levels and problems outside of the "normal" range, and to determine intervention goals that are developmentally relevant rather than simply satisfying adult expectations.

One instrument that is both strength-based and developmentally sequenced is the *Behavioral Objective Sequence* (Braaten 1998). While it was developed and refined over a 20-year period and has been used for several years, little research has been conducted to investigate the validity of BOS ratings for students with EBD (Bloomberg & Braaten, 1989). The *Behavioral Objective Sequence* (BOS) consists of 233 developmentally sequenced and measurable social competencies that may be assessed through structured observation and/or by ratings of multiple sources. The BOS is a skill- or strength-based tool rather than a problem- or deficit-based instrument. Further, it provides goals and objectives for the development and implementation of intervention curriculum derived directly from a current performance assessment.

The combination of the CARE and the BOS can be a powerful guide

to help youth mature in a healthy manner. The CARE provides risk assessment and a case management plan, while the BOS provides very
specific details on how to build healthy skills.

An Exercise to Assess Where the Youth Sees Him/Herself in the Attachment Process

After extensive work in the field, I found that I needed a concrete
way for the child, family, and therapist to communicate where they
are in the process of forming healthy attachments with each other. I
devised and have used the following exercise many times with great
success. This exercise is an interactive one between therapist, child,
and family. Draw a curved line, similar to a large cursive "U" on a
sheet of paper (see Drawing 1). Tell the child that this is how it feels
when you have attachment problems. It's like you are in a hole away
from everyone and no one can help you. Have the child draw himself
at the bottom of the curve of the "U." Place yourself (or foster parents, grandparents, adoptive parents, etc.) up on the ledge waiting
for a way to get the child to come up and attach to you (have child or
caregiver draw the adults on the ledge). Ask the child, *How will you
reach me/them? It seems like a very big hole.* Let the child propose a
few ways, and passively say that you hear his suggestions — and that
those might be possibilities.

Then say, *Therapy is like having me place a ladder down in this hole
for you to use* (draw a ladder from the bottom of the hole to the
ledge). *I can help you climb that ladder, but you have to do things
my way, let your parents be the bosses, follow their rules, and be
fun to be around. That doesn't sound like such a big thing, does*

it? But, you have to want to be up on the ledge with your (foster, adoptive, grand) parents for this to work. Do you really want to be part of this family? All youths for which I have used this have said yes. This process is an avenue for the youth and the family to communicate verbal commitment to the therapy "work" — an essential component to this type of therapy.

Have the youth draw himself where he thinks he is on the climb to attachment. I find that kids generally make very accurate assessments of where they are. I do this periodically to map progress for the child and the parents. It is important that it is a joint picture, with everyone contributing something, including the parents. It is also important to have the parents either confirm or disagree about where the child sees himself on the ladder, and allow everyone to have their own opinion. This will generate some discussion about progress and future goals, which is also essential to the process.

What would using the CARE during the adolescence of Ted Kaczynski and Charles Manson have told us? Using the CARE to score what is known about the childhoods of Kaczynski and Manson, Kaczynski has a CARE score of 0, indicating a lack of externalizing behavior problems in adolescence, but a 4 on the Psychiatric subscale, indicating that a major mental illness is likely. Manson scored a 36 on the CARE, indicating severe externalizing behavior problems in adolescence, but not signs of a major mental illness. Using the subscales for attachment problems and chronic violence in childhood and adolescence, Kaczynski was not similar to youths with problems associated with disrupted attachment patterns or chronic violence in childhood, but Manson was.

The CARE shows that the services needed for Kaczynski during childhood and adolescence were a psychiatric evaluation, social skills work using CBT, and family therapy. Services needed for Manson were CBT skill-building activities, a structured environment, therapy for attachment and trauma issues, a mental health evaluation, family therapy, and a substance abuse evaluation followed by substance abuse education or treatment as needed. He was similar to those with severe behavior problems, severe risk for future violence, and the need for residential placement. With the CARE, we would have known that Kaczynski had a major mental illness that needed to be treated, and that he was not at a high risk for violence as a youth. We would have known that Manson had chronic and severe externalizing behavior problems that needed appropriate therapy and a residential placement, and that he was at very high risk for violence as a youth. It appears that Kaczynski did not have attachment problems, while Manson did have those problems. They both needed treatment, but the interventions for the two, if carried out, would have been very different.

Chapter 7

Assessing Severe, Chronic Aggression and Psychopathy

What are the characteristics of those plagued with severe and chronic aggressive behaviors? What is the role of Attachment Disorder and Psychopathy in the development of violent behaviors? Part II will attempt to answer these questions and give us the knowledge and tools necessary to assess the varying risk factors.

In his 1979 book, *The Making and Breaking of Affectional Bonds*, John Bowlby stated, "In psychopaths, the incidence of illegitimacy and the shunting of the child from one home to another is high." He concluded, as I discussed in previous chapters, that the disruption of bonding produces a person incapable of feeling empathy, affection, or remorse (Newton 2000).

Adult male violence has been extensively studied. While it has declined since 1994, it still remains a significant problem. Risk and resiliency factors have been identified and risk tools have been created and studied for many years. Factors contributing to risk of future violence include past violence, employment problems, and skill deficits. There appear to be two types of adult male violence:

hot and cold. Hot violence derives from anger, while cold violence derives from cold-blooded psychopathy and/or sadism, as seen in Ted Bundy and David Berkowitz. Examples of both types of adult perpetrators can be found in every prison in the world.

The most recognized study of violence among those with a mental illness is the MacArthur Study (Monahan, Steadman, Silver, Appelbaum, Robbins, Mulvey, Roth, Grisso, Banks, 2001) In this longitudinal and cross-sectional study, mentally ill patients who were also substance abusers had the highest risk for violence. In fact, a diagnosis of schizophrenia without other risk factors was not a predictor of violence at all. This supports the idea that whatever causes people to be violent is a separate construct from mental illness; these constructs may co-occur in the same person, but the relationship is complex, not straightforward.

Intimate partner violence has also been well researched. The majority of intimate partner abusers are men, although one-third are women (Pennison and Welchans, 2000; http://www.ojp.usdoj.gov/bjs/pub/ascii/ipv.txt). This, however, is an under-publicized phenomenon, which I will pursue in my next book.

The backgrounds of 36 sexually-motivated killers (29 with multiple victims) were examined in an FBI study (Newton 2000) in an attempt to develop clues about indications of violent potential. The percentage with family histories of various characteristics are shown below.

Chart 5 — FBI study. Percent of Group: Family Characteristics of 36 Sexually-Motivated Killers (Murich, internet document; Newton, 2000)

- Alcohol abuse — 69%
- Psychiatric problems — 53%
- Criminal history — 50%
- Family sexual problems — 46%
- Family drug abuse — 33%
- History of psychological abuse — 74%
- Instability of home — 68%
- Lacks positive relationship with primary male care giver — 72%

Chart 6 — FBI Study. Common characteristics of 36 Sexually-Motivated Killers (Murich, internet document; Newton, 2000)

- Male — 100%
- Caucasian — 90%
- Average or better IQ — 80%
- History of physical abuse — 42%
- History of psychological abuse — 74%
- History of sexual abuse — 43%
- Sexual injury or disease — 28%
- History of sexually stressful events — 73%
- Childhood fetishism — 72%
- Childhood enuresis — 68%
- Childhood fire setting — 56%
- Tortured animals as children — 46%
- Cruel to childhood peers — 54%
- Chronic lying — 71%
- Assaulted adults in adolescence — 84%
- Dropped out of high school — 47%
- Persistent headaches — 29%
- Dressed as girls in childhood (some as a punishment to humiliate them) — 7%
- Psychopathic as measured by the PCL-R — 66%

Chart 7 — The FBI has also proposed the characteristics of the disorganized killer (Newton 2000):

- Below average to average IQ
- Socially immature
- Unstable work history of person and family
- Killer lives alone, is sexually incompetent or virginal
- Crimes are impulsive in nature
- Crimes are random
- Often knows his/her victim
- Disfigures or covers face of victim
- Little effort to conceal crime

Chart 8 — Other characteristics of Disorganized Killers Include (Newton 2000):

- Caucasian — 89%
- Have female victims — 65%
- Have victims of the opposite sex — 42%
- Choose victims of the same sex — 16%
- Has victims of both sexes — 39%
- Kills someone of the same race — 65%
- Only has victims of another race — 10%
- Kills both same and other ethnicities — 11%
- Victims are children or elderly — 6%

As we can see from the lists above, serial murderers and sexually motivated killers have multiple problems, just as the majority of the youths and adults presented in this book. It further supports the need for individual and family interventions in order to prevent future offending. This book proposes that the problems start early in life and the assessments and interventions should do likewise. The next section of this chapter will explore the tools available for assessing psychopathy in particular.

Assessing Psychopathy

Most of us are familiar with the infamous figures that we might assume are psychopaths. For instance, Ted Kaczynski, whose background was discussed in Chapter 3, had difficulty with interpersonal relationships, was violent, was irresponsible, and lacked empathy. However, he did not appear to have criminal versatility. We can assume he was self-centered and shallow, but without direct knowledge. But can we confirm this?

The background of Charles Manson was also discussed earlier in this book. He was self-centered, violent, lacked empathy, was highly manipulative,was shallow, and had multiple female relationships. In order to demonstrate the methods for determining psychopathy, I will discuss psychopathy and assessment tools in the following pages. Later in the chapter, I will score Kaczynski and Manson on the PCL-R as I did with the CARE earlier in the text. I will discuss what the findings of this mean for others in their work to prevent future violence.

Characteristics

Psychopathy was originally referred to as "moral insanity," "insanity without delirium," or "psychopathic inferiority." Then in 1941, Hervey Cleckley described psychopathy in *The Mask of Sanity*, giving us the language that we use today for this mental illness. He reported 16 traits that he believed to be associated with psychopathy, including manipulativeness, irresponsibility, self-centeredness, shallowness, lacking empathy or anxiety, criminal versatility, and violent offending. He also noted psychiatry's reluctance to deal with the diagnosis because of the difficulty of identifying it from outward symptoms.

Since that time, Dr. Robert Hare and Associates have thoroughly described psychopathy and created the Psychopathy Checklist-Revised (PCL-R). In 2005, Hare and Neumann proposed that four structures underlie the psychopathy construct: interpersonal, affect, lifestyle, and antisocial personality traits. It is hypothesized that psychopathy may be at the extreme end of a continuum of normal personality traits. Psychopathy can be more specifically described as disregarding the rights and feelings of others, manipulating and harming others to get what one wants, committing violence against others (sometimes sadistically so), being criminally diverse, and having a parasitically-oriented lifestyle. Examples include Ted Bundy, Son of Sam, John Wayne Gacy, and Jeffrey Dahmer. Blair et al. (2002) found that those adults scoring high on Hare's PCL-R were impaired in the recognition of fear responses in others. Thus, they lack an important violence-inhibiting personality structure.

Andersen et al. (1999) found that those who scored high on the PCL-R had chronic psychotic disorders at a greater frequency, exhibited previous suicide attempts, and were psychosocially maladjusted.

Psychopaths also have a reduced ability to exert behavioral patterns that suppress the dominant response (immediate gratification) and allow a secondary response (delayed gratification) when needed. This is associated with fearfulness and conscious development. So, if Johnny wants Sally's candy and she won't give him any, he can use the dominant response to take it, or suppress the dominant response and use a secondary response that takes Sally's needs and feelings into account: walk away, get his own candy, ask his mother, cry, etc. Psychopaths seem deficient in this area, in suppressing the dominant response in order to take the other person's feelings or needs into account. It is the Me, Me, Me! Syndrome: *Only what I want counts.* This is, again, a very early (egocentric) stage of moral development. Since psychopaths are also deficient in recognizing fear responses in others, they do not fully understand (or care) that they have harmed others to meet their own needs.

Barry et. al (2000) found that youths with ADHD, conduct disorder, or Oppositional Defiant Disorder (ODD) who also had callous and unemotional traits were less distressed by their misbehavior and lacked fearfulness, and were thus similar to adult psychopaths. They concluded that characteristics of psychopathy in youths appear to be similar to those found among psychopathic adults. However, they also concluded that diagnoses of ADHD, conduct disorder, or ODD are not sufficient to distinguish youths with psychopathic traits. It should be stressed that most children diagnosed with one of these disorders, especially those that live in nurturing, caring environments, may not develop any characteristics of psychopathy. These disorders are simply one of many factors that may come together to produce psychopathy if enough are present in the child's environment.

Neurobiology

Blair (2005) described the Integrated Emotion Systems (IES) model of the development of psychopathy. He proposes that the amygdala is a crucial area of the brain that processes emotion. Considerable MRI research supports the dysfunction of the amygdala (the area of the brain that processes emotions) in psychopathic individuals. This dysfunction interrupts aversive conditioning and the processing of emotional information, reduced startle reflex by visual threat, passive avoidance learning, and the recognition of fearful expressions in others. This causes the developing child to be less able to take advantage of moral social referencing and thus respond appropriately to the distress of others. Fearfulness, then, indexes the "integrity of the neural system necessary for empathy." It appears that the ability to respond to rewards is impaired, but less so than the ability to respond to punishment in "fearless children." This leads to the hypothesis that interventions that use positive maternal responsiveness and the formation of secure attachments may have promise when treating youths who are at risk for psychopathy. Conversely, lack of or dysfunctional attachment and lack of maternal responsiveness may be at the root of the development of psychopathy, which is why it is important to understand these characteristics of DAP.

Laakso, M.P. et al. (2001) found large negative correlations (-.79) between psychopathy measured by the PCL-R (Hare 1991) and volume of the posterior of the hippocampi (the two parts of the brain's limbic system that play a part in memory and spatial navigation) bilaterally measured by an MRI. The most likely outcome of this neuro-anatomical deficit would be impairment of the ability to develop conditioned fear, commonly seen among psychopaths.

It is likely that there is also a genetic component in the development of psychopathy that predisposes one to the callous, unemotional elements of psychopathy (Blair 2005). Early childhood stressors have significant effects on the hypothalamic-pituitary-adrenal axis activity and the generation of norepinephrine, as well. This also reduces the ability to learn appropriate social behaviors. Hare (1995) has adeptly described the inability of psychopaths to express the proper emotional state in facial expression and through tone of voice that is congruent with how they feel. They appear to learn the appropriate response for a particular situation. In other words, they are not responding to an internal state; they have learned facial expression and tonal quality that go with particular situations by watching what others do in those situations and mimicking them, without internalizing the emotions of the responses.

Precursors

Reid Meloy (2002) uses a review of the psychoanalytic and object relations literature to put forth a theory of the connection between disrupted attachment patterns and psychopathy. Additionally, Harris, Rice, and Lalumiere (2001) found that antisocial parenting is related to neurodevelopmental insult and psychopathy. Neurodevelopmental insults are not significantly associated with psychopathy, but both are significantly, directly, and independently related to criminal violence (see Figure 7.1). This supports the idea that psychopathy may be a life history strategy.

Figure 7. — Theoretical Model of the Development of Criminal Violence

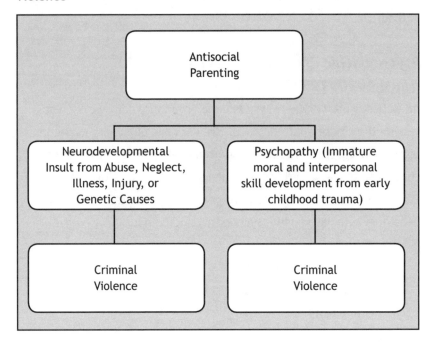

Marshall and Cooke (1999) also found that aversive family and societal experiences in childhood were highly correlated with psychopathic traits in adults when compared with lack of psychopathic traits in a control group of adults. Caputo, Frick, and Brodsky (1999) found that witnessing violence in childhood distinguished violent and sexual juvenile offenders from offenders with non-contact offenses.

Assessment

The PCL-R (Hare 1991) is the most widely accepted assessment of adult psychopathy. Hare (1991) noted that self-report inventories such as the MMPI and MCMI were insufficient to assess this population because of the lack of truthfulness that characterizes the population. Furthermore, the symptoms of psychopathy are more readily recognized within a social context, rather than in isolated individuals.

Psychopathic Checklist — Revised (PCL-R) (Hare 1990, 1991)

Dr. Robert Hare (1990, 1991) has done groundbreaking work on assessing the risk of adult violence. His work has been very useful in discriminating those with psychopathic traits, those at high risk for chronic violence, and those with little risk for violent offending. The PCL-R uses 20 items that measure personality characteristics and behaviors associated with psychopathy, including:

- Callous lack of empathy
- Manipulation of others for self-gain
- Grandiosity
- Need for stimulation
- Shallow affect
- Glibness/superficial charm
- Pathological lying
- Lack of remorse or guilt
- Parasitic lifestyle
- Poor behavioral controls
- Promiscuous sexual behavior
- Early behavior problems
- Lack of realistic, long-term goals
- Impulsivity
- Irresponsibility
- Failure to accept responsibility for one's actions
- Chronic criminal behavior

On its own, the PCL-R is a moderate predictor of both general and violent recidivism (Hemphill, Hare, and Wong 1998). However, Freedman (2001) found that the error rates of the PCL-R are too high to use it as a valid predictor of future violence. Correlations with actual violence are approximately .27. The PCL-R is the gold standard in assessing psychopathy. On a cautionary note, the PCL-R score has not been found to correlate with female violence. Psychopathy is a clinical construct and therefore relates to prevention and treatment methodologies. One explanation for the moderate correlation between the PCL-R and violence could be that not all psychopaths, particularly female psychopaths, are overtly violent. However, those that are violent are chronically violent. Perhaps there is a form of psychopathy that is violent toward others and one that is violent toward the self, or withdrawn from society altogether. More research may be needed to define typologies. Until then, the PCL-R will continue to be used by many for clinical purposes.

As seen in Figure 7.2, there are similar items in the Hare Psychopathy Checklist and my CARE Attachment Subscale (Seifert 2006). This demonstrates that those with psychopathy and disrupted attachment share some of the same traits. In an examination of the CARE data, the association between clinically diagnosed attachment problems and PCL-YV scores for 21 youths were significant (r =.73, p = .01).

Figure 7.2 – Comparison of Assessments for Sociopathy and Conduct Disorder

Assessment of Disrupted /Disorganized Attachment Patterns (ADDAP) DISORGANIZED ATTACHMENT	CARE (Seifert, 2003) Attachment Subscale DISORGANIZED ATTACHMENT	PCL-YV (Forth, Hasson, 2003) PSYCHOPATHY-YOUTH	DSM-IV – Conduct Disorder CONDUCT DISORDER	PCL-R (Hare 1991) PSYCHOPATHY-ADULT	DSM-IV (sociopathy) SOCIOPATHY	Number of instruments with similar criteria
Lacks remorse	Lacks remorse	Lack of remorse		Lacks remorse	Lack of remorse, as indicated by being indifferent about having hurt, mistreated, or stolen from another	Attachment, Sociopathy, and Psychopathy-Adult
Very Charming when it suits his or her purposes		Impression management		Glib/Superficially Charming		Attachment and Psychopathy
Pathological Lying		Pathological Lying	Deceitfulness to obtain goods or favors	Pathological Lying	Deceitfulness	Attachment, CD, Sociopathy, and Psychopathy
Manipulative of others for self gain		Manipulation for Personal Gain		Manipulative of others for self gain		Attachment and Psychopathy
Severe Behavior Problems	Severe Behavior Problems		Repetitive and persistent pattern of violation of the Basic rights of others and societal rules.	Poor Behavioral Control	Repetitive and persistent pattern of violation of the Basic rights of others and societal rules.	Attachment, CD, Sociopathy, and Psychopathy-Adult

Early Behavior Problems	Early Behavior Problems		Early Behavior Problems		Attachment and Psychopathy
Impulsivity	Impulsivity		Impulsivity	Impulsivity or failure to plan ahead	Attachment, Sociopathy, and Psychopathy
Violent, aggressive		Often Initiates physical fights; Has used a weapon that can cause serious physical harm to others; Has been physically cruel to people	Violent	Irritability and aggressiveness, as indicated by repeated physical fights or assaults	Attachment, CD, Sociopathy, and Psychopathy-Adult
Childhood Trauma	Childhood Trauma				Attachment
Emotionally Cold, Extreme or lack of expression of emotion or shallow emotional expression	Shallow Affect		Shallow Affect		Attachment and Psychopathy
Bullying Behavior	Bullies, threatens, or intimidates others	Pervasive pattern of disregard for, and violation of, the rights of others			Attachment, CD, Sociopathy, and Psychopathy
Self-centered	Parasitic Orientation		Parasitic Lifestyle		Attachment and Psychopathy

	Serious Criminal Behavior; Criminal Diversity	Criminal Diversity		
	Serious Criminal Behavior; Criminal Diversity			Psychopathy
	Grandiose sense of self worth	Grandiose sense of self worth		Psychopathy
	Stimulation seeking	Risk Taker, Need for stimulation	Reckless disregard for safety of self or others	Psychopathy and Sociopathy
Lacks Empathy	Callous lack of Empathy	Callous lack of Empathy		Attachment and Psychopathy
	Irresponsibility	Irresponsibility	Consistent irresponsibility, as indicated by repeated failure to sustain consistent work behavior or honor financial obligations	Psychopathy and Sociopathy
	Impersonal Sexual Behavior	Promiscuous sexual behavior		Psychopathy
	Lacks Goals	Lack of realistic, long term goals		Psychopathy
Does not accept responsibility for actions	Failure to accept Responsibility for Actions	Failure to accept responsibility for one's action		Attachment and Psychopathy
	Poor Anger Control			Psychopathy – Juvenile

	Unstable Interpersonal Relationships / Serious Violations of Conditional Release		Unstable Interpersonal Relationships	Attachment and Psychopathy
Poor social skills				Psychopathy
Harms animals		Has been physically cruel to animals		Attachment and CD
History of Violence		Has stolen while physically confronting a victim		CD and Attachment
		Has Forced Someone into Sexual Activity		
Fire Setting		Has deliberately engaged in fire setting with the intention of causing serious damage to another's		Attachment and CD
Stealing		Property Stealing		Attachment and CD

		Runaway, Truant, stays out at night despite parental prohibition			Attachment and CD
Truant, curfew violations					
Severely deficient problem-solving skills					Attachment
Lack of commitment to education					Attachment
Family History of Violence					Attachment
Family has low warmth and high conflict					Attachment
Caregiver(s) has(ve) history of psychiatric problems or substance abuse					Attachment
One or both parents dead, addicted, incarcerated or otherwise uninvolved in child's life					Attachment

There are 35 traits found for descriptions of disorganized attachment, conduct disorder, sociopathy, and psychopathy assessments. Eighteen of the 35 items are found on attachment, conduct disorder, and psychopathy/sociopathy measures. An additional six of the "psychopathy only" items are also characteristic of youth with attachment disorders.

Below is a list of items that the PCL-YV, PCL-R and ADDAP have in common:

- Lacks remorse
- Superficially charming (impression management)
- Pathological lying
- Manipulative for self-gain
- Early behavior problems
- Impulsivity
- Shallow affect (emotionally cold)
- Lacks empathy
- Does not accept responsibility for actions

Charles Manson had eight of the above items, while Ted Kaczynski had only three of the items. Unless new information comes to light, it is not likely that Kaczynski was a psychopath or had disrupted attachment patterns, but Charles Manson had the characteristics of both. Based on the above criteria, it is likely that Ted Bundy was a psychopath, as well, because he had seven of the above characteristics. Most people usually have only up to two of these traits and no history of engaging in violence. For instance, my son, John, has none of the above characteristics, was raised in a positive, loving environment, and has never been violent. Another relative, however, was raised in a home with domestic violence. He has seven of the above characteristics and has exhibited some moderate violence.

Dr. Hare (1991) and others have suggested that psychopathy is different from sociopathy and may be an extreme form of antisocial personality disorder. In fact, Dr. Hare tried to provide information to the Diagnostic and Statistical Manual of Mental Disorders Committee (or DSM, a comprehensive classification of officially recognized psychiatric disorders published by the American Psychiatric Association used by mental health professionals to ensure uniformity of diagnosis) about psychopathy. However, the committee decided that they would only use items that could be reliably measured, and did not distinguish psychopathy from sociopathy.

At the very least, this indicates that psychopathy and attachment problems have 18 to 24 out of 35 traits in common. Are they the same disorder? If not the same disorder, are they variations of each other or could they be overlapping disorders? It will take more research to determine this. Of course, any disorder is going to have a different presentation in childhood than it would in adulthood, hence the differences between the two scales. One of the conceptual differences between the PCL and the ADDAP is the idea that attachment problems, which are a result of pathological caregiving early in life, are important to understanding, assessing, and ultimately treating the disorder. However, there is research evidence that adult psychopathy may be linked to pathological caregiving at an early age, thus the possible link between attachment problems in childhood and psychopathy in adulthood. If research supports this link, it would give us the keys to early prevention of psychopathy, which may lie in strengthening the public child welfare, mental health, and juvenile justice systems.

Chapter 8

Assessment of Behavior Problems, Violence, and Placement Needs

It is not sufficient to assess one family member and expect to get the full picture of individual characteristics and environmental dynamics that may be playing a part in the situation or problems to be solved. Assessments should be multifaceted and include the whole family.

I recently assessed a youth and his family for level of risk. The youth had not yet — to our knowledge — done anything that had come to the attention of the local authorities. Despite this, I determined by using the CARE that his level of risk was high. The social worker subsequently went to his home and found weapons and bomb-making material in the garage. We later found out that he had planted a pipe bomb near a school. He initially refused to tell authorities where the bomb was hidden, but he then relented to the relief of all concerned.

Another teen who had been having major problems at home, in school, and in the community was given the test and found to have a high CARE score. Unfortunately, because the recommended treatment was not pursued in time, he went on to torture, then butcher, a litter of kittens. Another youth with a high risk score is facing life in prison as an adult for a vicious rape. All of these stories serve as examples that the risk of future violence to be committed by youth can be reduced by using appropriate risk tools and ensuring that those at risk receive the services they need. This means, as I repeatedly have stressed throughout this book, that we need to invest adequate resources to do this very important job in a timely and effective manner.

Collection of Background Information

A complete psychological/risk evaluation balances youth and family needs with public safety. Children and teens that are at risk for violent offending have problems in multiple domains, such as in school and the community, with peers, and at home. Tolan and Guerra (1994) found that multifaceted assessment and treatment for juveniles with severe behavioral problems can be effective. This means that a good assessment should encompass an evaluation of all possible problem areas, such as school behavior, learning problems, psychiatric symptoms, trauma, legal issues, family problems, substance abuse, and skill areas. A good history will include child and family history of family violence, mental illness, substance abuse, child abuse, and criminality. It is important to assess and record attachment disorder indicators such as severe and chronic emotional and physical neglect in the first five years of life.

Neurological indicators include history of head injury, severe physical abuse, neglect, sustained high fevers in infancy and early childhood, ingestion of lead, maternal substance abuse during pregnancy, and child substance abuse. Psychiatric problems such as depression, anxiety, panic attacks, hallucinations, severe mood swings, explosive behavior, and dissociation also need to be assessed by a mental health professional. A psychosocial form can help systematize data collection. Multiple sources and types of data are also important. All aspects of a child's life, including school, home, community, friends, recreation, job, mental health, substance abuse, and history of offenses, need to be analyzed, as does information from all agencies involved in the case. Additionally, assessment of risk level can determine the needed intensity of services, from out-patient to secure residential settings.

Observation of the youth's behavior is also always important. I was called to assess a teenager who had exhibited inappropriate sexual touching of another. When he was brought into the room, he proceeded to run in circles while making grunting noises and "flapping" his hands. Staff could not get him to stop, and he was ushered out of the room. This was a clear diagnostic indicator that he should be evaluated for an autism spectrum disorder. It is cases such as these, in which conditions like autism are missed for so long, that speak to a true lack of training of professionals and educating parents in the area of autism spectrum disorders. Luckily, autism awareness seems to be increasing; there are television ads about it this year as part of a very good public information campaign. Perhaps with more awareness, acceptance, and information, these diagnoses will not be missed so often in the future.

A good psychosocial form can assist a worker in collecting necessary information on a youth and his/her family in a methodical way. (For sample psychosocial forms see my eBook available at *http://www.DrKathySeifert.com.*) The form will be slightly different for the adults, children and teens, and infants and toddlers. Categories should include:

- Description of the client, such as demeanor, cooperation, and ability to follow directions.
- Presenting the problem. What brought the person to the clinic in his own words?
- History of presenting problem. What are the various problems and how long have they been going on?
- Other agencies involved with the family. Is a public agency involved and for what reason(s)?
- Current living status. Who has custody? Are there any visitation arrangements? (The person(s) who have custody must sign the consent for treatment when the client is a juvenile.)
- Family members in the household and their names and ages.
- Client and family history of mental illness, substance abuse, criminality, or violence.
- Client educational history: school, class, grades, behavior.
- Social functioning: pro-social or deviant peers, loner or gregarious, or just a few friends.
- Developmental history: On time, any abnormalities?
- Complications of pregnancy or birth.
- Significant family events.
- Trauma history.
- Symptom check list.
- Mental health treatment history.
- Expectations of treatment.
- Medical history.
- Substance use by client and family.
- Legal status.

- Resources and assets.
- Mental status.
- Diagnosis.
- Comments or observations.

Psychosexual Assessment

Professionals often assume that only a small group of juveniles has sexual boundary or sexual offending problems, and therefore that the child they're working with doesn't have sexual problems. The reality is that many youth who come to the attention of the juvenile justice and child welfare systems have sexual victimization, boundary, or offending issues. Because youth will be reluctant to be forthcoming with information about sexual problems and many adults will find it difficult to discuss these topics, it is important to assess that area specifically, directly, and methodically. It is not enough to assess only the youths with known sexual behavior problems. In a recent study, high levels of comorbidity were found between violence, delinquency, fire-setting, and sexual behavior problems (Seifert 2006). Inquiring about sexual behavior problems among all youth with severe behavior problems should be routine.

This section will address some of the important questions to ask when conducting such an assessment. In addition to all of the above, the worker should include:

- Sexual history.
- Sexual victimization.
- Exposure to pornography.
- Sexual behaviors that have caused problems.
    - Youth accepts responsibility for these behaviors.

       — Youth can describe what happened and discuss it.
       — Family not in denial about the problems.
       — Youth and family willing to positively engage in therapy
          to change problem.
       — Youth and family have empathy for any (alleged) victim.
• Family members with sexual behavior problems.

The worker must be willing to talk frankly about these issues without embarrassment. Screening tools that are being researched for use in this area include the JSOAP, JRAT, and the ERASOR. These are guided interview instruments and none have a standardized scoring system or treatment planning guides. The CARE Sexual Behavior Problems Subscale uses both static and dynamic risk factors, is validated, and has a case management planning tool.

Assessment of Youth Violence Risk

Risk for violence and sexual offending are entirely different constructs than mental health issues, and they must be assessed separately. Determination of future risk of violence can contribute to decisions about the appropriate level of care or structure. Additionally, clinical judgment about the risk of future violence or sexual offending is only slightly better than chance. For that and many other reasons, any tools used to determine the fate of children and teens should have established reliability and validity. Tools developed to date to determine youth risk of future violence, delinquency, and behavior problems include the SAVRY, PCL-YV, YLS-CMI, CARE, RSTI, and the DVI. There is a lot of literature to indicate that self-report instruments are problematic with this population due to deceitfulness.

Drawing 1. Assessing Progress in Attachment to Caregivers

Where are you on the ladder?

parents

youth

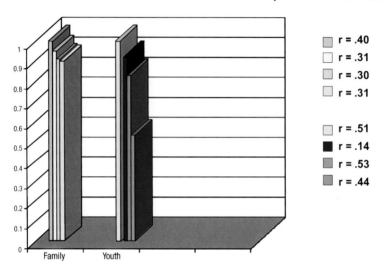

Figure 2. Characteristics of Sample Youth with Disrupted Attachment Patterns

Abbreviations:

r = correlation

Family

☐ r = .40 Family Violence (past or present)

☐ r = .31 Low Family Warmth/ High Conflict (past or present)

☐ r = .30 Family psychiatric or substance abuse problems (past or present)

☐ r = .31 Disciplinary practices of one or both parents are harsh, lax, or inconsistent (past or present)

Youth

☐ r = .51 Maltreatment before the age of 5 (past)

■ r = .14 Youth has symptoms of a psychiatric disorder (past or present)

☐ r = .53 Youth has history of assaultive behavior(s) (past or present)

☐ r = .44 Youth has delinquent actions – stealing, shoplifting, curfew or drug offences, etc. (past or present)

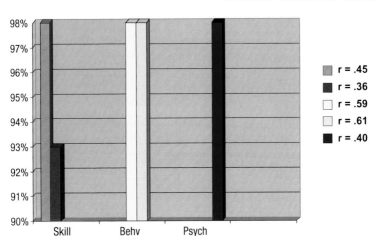

Figure 2.1. Problems of a Sample Youth with Disordered Attachment Patterns

Abbreviations:

r = correlation

Skill = Social deficits

r = .45 Social Skills

r = .36 Anger Management Problems

Behv = Behavior Problems

r = .59 Severe Behavior Problems

r = .61 Behavior Problems before the age of 12

Psych = Psychiatric Problems

r = .40 Implusive

Behavior is a Function of
Environment and Person (Lewin 1943)

Diagram 1

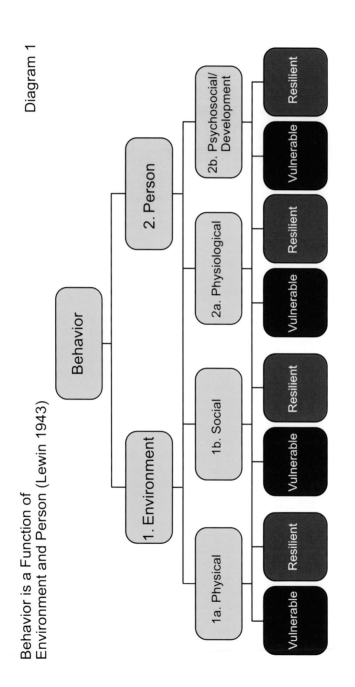

More detail on this model follows.

Physical Environment

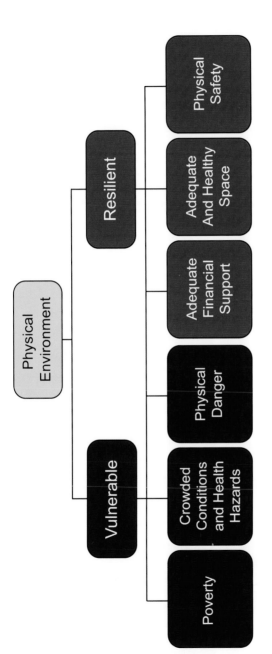

More detail on this model follows.

Development of the Person

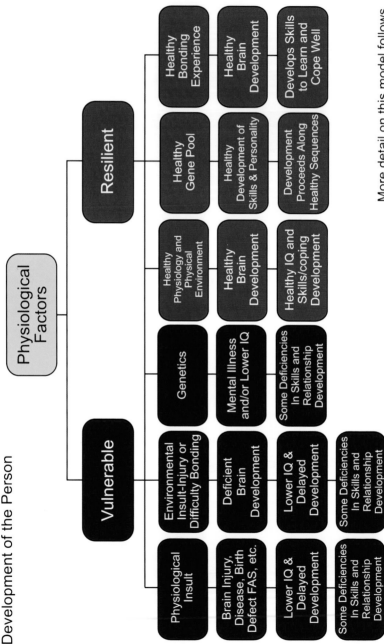

More detail on this model follows.

Social Environment

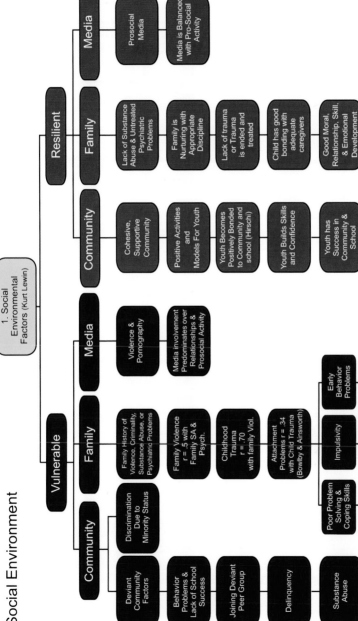

More detail on this model follows.

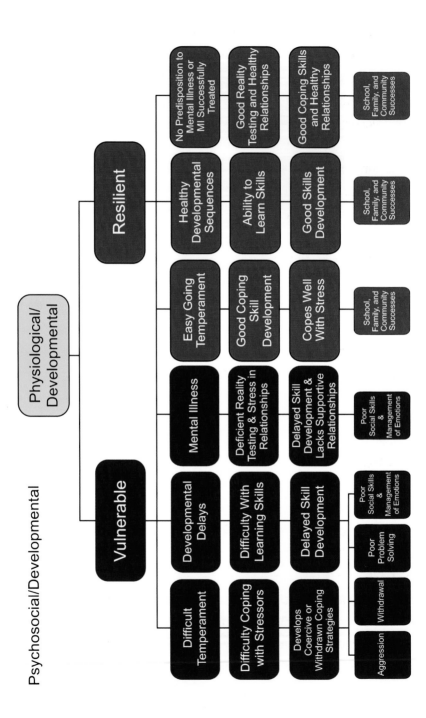

The Hare Psychopathy Check List: Youth Version (PCL: YV) (Forth, Kosson, and Hare 2003)

The PCL: YV assesses psychopathic traits in 12- to 18-year-old offenders. While Drs. Forth, Kosson, and Hare believe that identifying youth with psychopathic traits is critical to understanding the factors that contribute to the development of adult psychopathy, the application of the concept of psychopathy to youth is very controversial. For professional scoring the youth PCL uses an interview guide, then gathers collateral information to fill out the forms. The PCL: YV measures interpersonal, affective, and behavioral characteristics believed to be associated with psychopathy.

The Structured Assessment of Violence Risk in Youth (SAVRY) (Borum, Bartel, and Forth 2002)

There are 24 risk factors and 6 protective factors on the SAVRY. Each risk item can be scored on a three-point scale (High/Moderate/Low), while each protective factor has a two-level scoring structure (Present/Absent). Drs. Borum, Bartel, and Forth include both static and dynamic risk factors because of changes that typify adolescence. The SAVRY uses the concept of risk management needs, rather than specific prediction of future risk.

The Child and Adolescent Risk Evaluation (CARE) (Seifert 2003)

The CARE is an assessment of risk for violence that evaluates all possible problem areas, including past behavior, community, family, peer, job/school, neurological, and mental health. It is the first assessment tool that I developed, and an easy one to use for assessing the risk of youth violence and creating a multifaceted case management plan. The CARE draws upon information from multiple sources and assesses both risk and protective factors. The significance of the development of a tool such as the CARE is widespread, as it offers an opportunity for school, social service, criminal justice, and mental health professionals to access a reliable tool for determining the need for additional testing and for specific treatment protocols. As with the more commonly known adult actuarial risk tools, the CARE is based on the idea that the more risk factors an offender has, the greater his risk for recidivism. No one factor predicts youth violence. Each additional factor increases the risk that a youth will be violent, but individual factors have different weights. The CARE has a case management tool to determine the intensity and type of services needed for effective risk management.

The total CARE score appears to be significantly associated with a history of assaults (r = 62. p=.00; ROC = .87) and assaults committed after the administration of the instrument (r = .62, p=.00). Split half reliability is .85 and test-retest reliability is .75. Sample is 905.

CARE Chronic Violence Subscale

Through a statistical analysis of the data on the original CARE items, I selected and weighted the strongest predictors of chronic violence. Items included history of violence, behavior problems, harming animals, behavior problems before the age of 12, impulsivity, delinquency, lack of remorse, belief in the legitimacy of aggression as a means to an end, and other items. The sample size is 892 youths. While the original CARE measured the presence of any assaults, the Chronic Assault Subscale measured chronic assaultive behavior, defined as more than three unprovoked, non-self-defensive assaults on others. Twenty-seven percent of the sample (243) had a history of chronic assaultive behavior, while 57 percent of the sample (521) had at least one assault on another. When comparing the Chronic Subscale Total Score and the Chronic Assault variable, the statistics were strong (n = 911; Eta = .69; Eta2 = .48; F = 821.28, p = .00; ROC = .94 see Figure 2). For comparison, the ROC's for clinical judgment, the SAVRY and the PCL-YV are .51, .79, and .63-.79, respectively. While the original CARE is the best tool for the Case Management Plan, many may want to assess chronic violence risk rather than risk of any violent act and should use the Chronic Violence Subscale.

Risk Sophistication Treatment Inventory (RSTI) (Randall Salekin, University of Alabama, 2004)
The RSTI was normed on 591 youthful offenders ages 9 to 18. The sample included first-time and repeat offenders. The scale is a semi-structured interview with 45 items using a 32-page interview book. Areas assessed include risk for dangerousness, sophistication/maturity, and amenability to treatment. Items include past violent behavior, remorse levels, violence toward animals, conflict resolution, and interpersonal skills.

The Domestic Violence Inventory-Juvenile (DVI-J) (Behavior Data Systems, Ltd. 1996)
The DVI-J evaluates youth who have been accused or convicted of domestic violence. Scales include truthfulness, alcohol and drug use, violence (lethality), control, and stress coping scales. It is a self-report instrument with all of the problems associated with self-report. Behavior Data Systems reports one study on the DVI-J. I have used the DVI-J from time to time as an extra tool to compare with other results. It is quick and easy and it has a validity scale, but I find that juvenile justice populations are sometimes able to fool it.

Tests Not Correlated With Risk of Violence

Traditional tests, such as the MMPI-A, Rorschach, TAT, and the MACI, were not created for nor have they been evaluated in terms of their association with risk of violence. Additionally, popular tools, such as the CAFAS (Hodges 1990, 1994, 2003), CALOCUS (American Association of Community Psychiatrists 1999) and MAYSI (Grisso et al. 2001) do not assess risk for violence. I never use these instruments to determine risk of violence because they are not validated for this. However, I may use them for other reasons.

Behavioral Health and Recidivism Assessments

The Youth Level of Service/Case Management Inventory (YLS/CMI) (Hogue and Andrews 1996)

The YLS/CMI measures risk, need, and responsivity factors among adolescents ages 12 to 17 who had come in contact with the juvenile justice system. Its 42 items encompass eight scales: prior and current offenses, family circumstances, education/employment, peer relations, substance abuse, leisure/recreation, personality/behavior, and attitude/orientation. It is designed to be used by mental health professionals, drawing information from multiple sources. The results are used to formulate a level of risk and a specific treatment plan. I do not use the YLS/CMI, because the validity statistics in regard to recidivism are low to moderate.

EARL-20B (Augimeri et al. 1998, 2000)

The EARL-20B measures the potential for severe behavior problems among children ages 7 to 12 using a clinical interview guide. Items are scored from 0 to 2. The items are divided into three categories: Child, Family, and Responsivity. Interventions are also not included. Reliability is reported to be .93, and while validity statistics were not found in the literature, a study is underway. Visit *http://www.earlscourt.on.ca/docs/EARL_20B_1.pdf* for more information.

EARL 21G (Augimeri et al. 2002)

The EARL 21G is a 21-item assessment of behavioral problems among girls. The items are divided into Child, Family, and Responsivity. Reliability is good, but validity studies have not yet been reported. See this website for more information: *http://www.sfu.ca/gap/conferences/2002/levene.pdf*. Although I like their structure and items, I do not use the Earl instruments because validity research is still underway. Looking at the items, I suspect the validity will be good for behavior problems.

Jesness Inventory. (Jesness, C. 1988, Manual Rev. 1996)

The Jesness measures conduct and antisocial behaviors in youth. Scales include Social maladjustment, Value Orientation, Immaturity, Autism, Alienation, Manifest Aggression, Withdrawal/Depression, Social Anxiety, Repression, and Denial, and there is an asocial index. The website (*http://vinst.umdnj.edu/VAID/TestReport.asp?Code=JI*) states that the sample of over 3,000 was collected in the early 1960s. It contains 155 true/false items and requires a professional with a master's degree to score it. Validity is reported to be acceptable. I used the Jesness at one time, but now find other tools more useful for psychological evaluations.

JIFF (Hodges 2004)

The JIFF is a structured interview given to the caregiver of a youth that has come to the attention of a government agency. At the writing of this book, Dr. Hodges reported (2006 APA Conference in New Orleans) that there were two studies of the JIFF. One had a sample of 70 and the other had a sample of 155. There are ten domains of functioning (approximately five questions each): School, Home, Community, Behavior toward others, Moods/emotions, Self-harmful behavior, Substance use, Thinking, Family life, and Child health. It is not considered to be a professional or comprehensive assessment tool, but rather a screening tool to see if further assessment is needed. Items are rated on a 0 to 5 scale. This instrument appears to be useful and to have face validity, but needs a larger sample. More information can be found on the web at *http://rtckids.fmhi.usf. edu/rtcconference/19thconference/agenda/19th_handouts/pdf/Session%2044/Shackelford_babysteps.pdf*.

CANS (Leon et al. 1999)

The CANS measures dimensions of youth behavior, problems and strengths, family functioning, caregiver capacity, and care needs. It is intended to be a guide to service delivery for youth in the public mental health, juvenile justice, and social services systems. The authors state that it is face valid, easy to use, and comprehensive. Information can be found on the web (*http://www.buddinpraed.org/cans/*).

Mental Health/Psychiatric Assessment

CARE Psychiatric Subscale

The psychiatric subscale contains items such as paranoia, psychosis/self-harm, impulsivity, and flat or out-of-control emotions. Nine hundred eleven youth are in the sample. Eighty-three percent (758) of the youth in the sample have psychiatric problems and 17 percent (153) do not. The relationship between the total psychiatric score and clinician assessed psychiatric problems is: eta = .69; eta2 = .47; p = .00; F = 816.45; ROC = .96. By contrast, the Total Psychiatric subscale score is not significantly related to neurological disorders or youth with greater than three assaults. The score relates to the severity of the disorder and the level of therapy that might be needed. Severe psychiatric disorder means severe Axis I major mental illness that requires an assessment by a therapist and a psychiatrist.

The CARE and its subscales are used with every psychological assessment given by my agency, Eastern Shore Psychological Services. I find them to be indispensable in determining intervention plans. This scale helps determine the presence of psychiatric disorders in juvenile justice populations.

Massachusetts Assessment and the Massachusetts Youth Screening Instrument, Version 2 (MAYSI) (Grisso and Quinlan 2001)

The MAYSI has 52 items at a fifth-grade reading level. It is a true/false, self-report instrument measuring events and behaviors of the last few months. Subscales include: Alcohol/Drug Abuse, Angry/Irritable, Depressed/Anxious, Somatic Complaints/Suicidal Ideation, Thought Disturbances, and Traumatic Experiences. The substance abuse, trauma, suicidality, and anger scales were highly correlated with each other. The possibility of false negatives on the depression scale should also be kept in mind. The authors state that this is not a definitive tool for diagnosis, but it identifies those who need further evaluation. Information can be found here: *http://www.assessments. com/catalog/MAYSI_2.htm.*

Child Behavior Check List (CBCL) (Achenbach 1991)

This instrument is for youth ages 4 to 18 (there are separate scoring forms for 4 to 11 and 12 to 18). There are parent and teacher rating forms and youth self-report forms. The CBCL measures the social, emotional, and behavior problems of youth in the last six months. Reliability is reported to be good. For more information go to *http:// depts.washington.edu/soccomm/tests/cbcl.html.* The CBCL has been useful in my research and in the school-based mental health programs.

Conners' Rating Scale — Revised (CRS—R) (Conners 1997)

The Conners' Rating Scale assesses ADD/ADHD symptoms and other behavior problems among youth ages 3 to 17. There are parent, youth, and teacher report forms. With this instrument, clinicians can monitor a youth's progress in therapy or during the use of medication regimens. The long form includes the following scales: Oppositional, Social Problems, Cognitive Problems/Inattention, Psychosomatic, Hyperactivity, DSM-IV Symptom Subscales, Anxious-Shy, ADHD Index, Perfectionism, and the Conners' Global Index. I find the Conners, which has been validated with significant research, extremely helpful in determining diagnosis and treatment options, especially for ADD/ADHD.

Behavior Assessment System for Children (BASC — 2) (Reynolds and Kamphaus 2004)

The BASC-2 assesses the emotional and behavioral disorders of children, adolescents, and young adults (ages 2 to 25). It includes parent, teacher, and youth rating scales, a structured developmental history, and a form for behavioral observation. I have found the BASC-2 to be a very useful tool to use for assessing overall mental and behavioral health issues. More information can be found here: *http://www.agsnet.com/psych/oct04a.asp*.

Millon Adolescent Clinical Inventory (MACI) (Millon 1993, 2006)

The MACI is a self-report instrument with a sixth-grade reading level. There are validity scales that help override attempts to "fool" the test. The MACI is based on Millon's personality theory that was originally applied to adults. I find this instrument useful to some aspects for an assessment of criminal justice populations. I use this instrument for personality traits on Axis II, although I never diagnose a teenager with a personality disorder. It is shorter than the MMPI-A and I find the descriptions to be quite accurate most of the time. However, I never use self-report instruments as the only source of information in a psychological evaluation.

Millon Pre-Adolescent Clinical Inventory (M-PACI) (Millon et al. 2005)

The M-PACI is based on similar theoretical constructs as Millon's other instruments and identifies emerging personality styles. It is intended for use with children ages 9 to 12. I have used this instrument a few times and found it useful for developing intervention strategies. It is a newer instrument, so I have less experience with it. Find more on this test on the Web (*http://www.millon.net/instruments/MPACI.htm*).

Minnesota Multiphasic Personality Inventory — Adolescent (MMPI-A) (Butcher 1992)

The MMPI has been around for a long time; the Adolescent version is somewhat newer. Peer-reviewed studies of these instruments are numerous. The MMPI-A is very long, and sustaining attention for young adolescents and juvenile justice populations is sometimes difficult. I only use it if I suspect an Axis I disorder, such as a Mood Disorder or Schizophrenia. It also has a substance abuse scale that is helpful. Find more information on the Web (*http://www1.umn.edu/mmpi/*).

Assessment for Attachment and Complex PTSD

Neither the disorder of nor the assessment for attachment problems is well-researched, and there is much controversy in the field over theory, assessment, and treatment. Therefore, any action taken in this area should be treated with caution.

CARE Attachment Problems Subscale

Attachment Problems are less well-known than violence or sexual behavior problems, but may be at the root of the more overt inappropriate social behaviors. Knowing when a child has disrupted attachment problems or trauma issues can guide treatment and hopefully prevent future violence and sexual offending. Like the other subscales, it is intended to be used with the original CARE to take advantage of the treatment planning aspects of that tool. The sample includes 823 youth. Items on this subscale are severely deficient problem-solving skills, history of attachment symptoms, bullying, early abuse and neglect, exposure to domestic violence, school difficulties, caregivers who have untreated psychiatric or substance abuse problems, and parental abandonment. Participation in a positive, pro-social activity is a protective factor. Statistical analysis was used to provide psychometric properties of the subscale. Those with mild to moderate scores may need family trauma therapy, while those with the highest scores will need trauma and attachment work as well as skill-building.

Trauma Symptom Check List for Children (TSCC) (Briere 1996)

The TSCC can be used with youths ages 8 to 16. It is a self-report measure of symptoms usually associated with post traumatic stress disorder. It is fairly transparent and has all the problems associated with self-report scales in juvenile justice populations. There are scales for under- and hyper-responding and one version has items related to sexual trauma. More product information can be found here: *http://www3.parinc.com/products/product.aspx?Productid=TSCC.*

I use the TSCC, but find it less useful for the juvenile justice youth who rarely admit to trauma symptoms, although most of them have experienced trauma.

Reactive Attachment Disorder Questionnaire RADQ (Randolph 1996)

The RADQ distinguishes between an attachment and a conduct disorder. It can be used for youth ages 5 to 18. There are three attachment subtypes: avoidant, anxious, or ambivalent. Very little peer-reviewed research on this tool is available. I rarely use it, as I find it cumbersome and that the theory behind it does not coalesce with my thinking. (*http://www.instituteforattachment.org/articles/article_41.htm*)

Assessment for Sexual Behavior Problems

Roger was tall, olive-skinned, and thin in build. He was raised by a violent, psychotic grandfather after his mother disappeared. He was severely abused and neglected, and was sexually abused by a relative. As a youth, he sexually abused his sister as well as a neighbor and was placed in a treatment center. While in treatment, he was extremely violent, but he did not have an opportunity to sexually offend. When he was released, he went to live with his grandfather once again. It was a volatile mix. After one year, his grandfather's house mysteriously burned to the ground, and Roger had to find a new place to live. After examining the characteristics of some of the evaluation tools, I will score him on two of the following assessments.

CARE Sexual Behavior Problems Subscale (SBP)

The SBP Subscale is intended to be used with the CARE and only with youths who have a history of sexually inappropriate behaviors. The items are: history of behavior problems, assaultive behavior, sexual assault of another, delinquency, and learning problems. The items were statistically determined and weighted on a sample of 905 youth. The sample contains 737 (81 percent) youths with no histories of sexually assaulting others and 168 (19 percent) who have sexually assaulted others. The statistics for this subscale are strong (Eta = .64; Eta2 = .41; p = .00; F = 628.11; ROC = .94; see Figure 3). Youths with low scores may just need some education and social skill development, those with mild to moderate scores will need further assessment to determine the types of therapy needed, and those with the highest scores will need therapy specifically related to sexual behavior problems. For more in-depth information on this topic, see *http://www.DrKathySeifert.com*.

Estimate of Risk of Adolescent Sexual Offence Recidivism (ERASOR) (Worling and Curwen 2001)

The ERASOR is a guided interview tool used to estimate the risk of juvenile sexual re-offense. It's used for youth ages 12 to 18 and includes both static and dynamic factors. This is a very nice structured interview process for gathering information about sexual behavior problems.

The Juvenile Risk Assessment Tool (JRAT)

The JRAT is one of a series of related structured clinical instruments used to assess risk for sexual re-offending in juvenile sexual offenders or ongoing sexually reactive behavior in children (including behavior that is sexually abusive to others). The tools are used by clinicians both to complete an initial assessment of and assign a level of risk (in juvenile sexual offenders) for sexual re-offense, as a structured means for evaluating response to treatment and the re-assessment of risk over time, and during treatment.

These instruments are empirically-based structured tools for clinical assessment. That is, the risk and other factors believed related to risk for continued sexually-abusive behavior are based on pertinent literature in the field, including published studies, and the instruments provided include defined factors to be addressed and a specific structure to be followed by the clinician completing the evaluation (Rich 2003).

The completion of the risk assessment tool first requires that the clinician gather a complete psychosocial history, based on record review, direct interviews with the child or adolescent, and interviews with collateral informants such as parents, teachers, therapists, social service agency workers, etc. (American Academy of Child and Adolescent Psychiatry 1999; National Task Force on Juvenile Sexual Offending 1993; Rich 2003).

The tools are used to assess behavior considered sexually reactive (including sexually abusive behavior) in children aged 9 to 13, the risk for sexual re-offense in juvenile sexual offenders and juvenile sexual offenders with cognitive impairments (such as mental retardation, borderline intellectual functioning, and neurological impairment). The JRAT, the CI/JRAT (Cognitively Impaired/Juvenile Risk Assessment Tool), and the LA-SAAT (Latency Age-Sexual Adjustment and Assessment Tool) and their ongoing re-assessment tools are available through the authors (Stetson School 2000). The JRAT series is also very nice for guided interviewing. The particularly nice thing about it is the breakdown of various ages and groups for more specific assessment (http://www.stetsonschool.org/Services/Assessment_Services/assessment_services.html).

The Juvenile Sex Offender Assessment Protocol-II (JJPI/JSOAP-II) (Prentky and Righthand 2003)

The JSOAP-II assesses risk factors that have been associated with sexual and criminal offending. The tool is appropriate for boys from 12 to 18 years of age who have had sexual behavior problems. The scale uses static and dynamic factors. There are four scales:

Scale I: Sexual Drive/Sexual Preoccupation
Scale II: Impulsive, Antisocial Behavior
Scale III: Clinical/Treatment
Scale IV: Community Adjustment

The last two scales are the two major dynamic areas that could assess behavior change, making them very useful. There have been peer-reviewed studies of this instrument (*http://www.csom.org/pubs/JSOAP.pdf*).

Sexual Adjustment Scale – Juvenile (SAI-J) (Behavior Data Systems)

The SAI-J is a self-report inventory of sexual behaviors. The report includes a risk management section with validity subscales. It has 195 items and can be used for youth 14 to 18 years of age. Psychometrics on this scale have not been found in the literature. I have found this scale useful for less sophisticated youth with sexual behavior problems (*http://www.bdsltd.com/index.htm*).

The Juvenile Sexual Offense Recidivism Risk Assessment Tool – JSORRAT-II (Epperson 2005)

The JSORRAT-II is the newest instrument for risk assessment. Research is ongoing and it shows much promise.

*   *   *

So let's score Roger on two of the above instruments and see what we find. Roger's score on the CARE sexual behavior subscale is nine. He is similar to other youth who are at severe risk for future sexual offending. On the CARE, his need for structure is high. Interventions needed include:

- Cognitive-behavioral treatment for social skills, problem solving, and anger management
- Therapy for early trauma
- Therapy for attachment issues
- Therapy specific to sexual behavior problems

The JSOAP II identifies items to be addressed in interventions. For Roger, some of these were:

- Sexual drive and pre-occupation
- History of sexual victimizatio
- Stability of current living situation
- Pervasive anger
- Difficulty managing anger
- Lack of evidence of support system

Despite his high risk score, Roger became too old to be eligible for the available residential treatment centers. He is therefore living out in the community, and without the proper resources, there is no way to find him and encourage him to enter treatment. Since there are not yet any new charges, treatment cannot be mandated. Chances that he will never have another violent or sexual offense are low. So we can only wait until that inevitable new charge. I hope I am wrong, but we cannot even provide preventive work to ensure there are no new charges. Hopefully one day there will be enough resources within the system to prevent future tragedies such as this one.

Assessment for Structure, Placement, and Treatment Needs

In a day when resources are very precious, it is increasingly more important to allocate high-cost resources for children who need them and not inappropriately for those who don't. While assessments for these purposes are not perfect, they do provide guidance in this process. Instruments include the CAFAS, CASII, CARE, and YLS/CMI.

The Child and Adolescent Functional Assessment Scale CAFAS (Hodges 1990, 1994, 2003)

The CAFAS assesses functional impairment among youth with emotional, behavioral, or substance use problems. The CAFAS is scored by clinicians to determine clinical progress or outcome. Scoring the scale for someone who knows the child well takes approximately 10 minutes. The CAFAS contains lists of behaviors and descriptions that are used to determine the youth's level of functioning. Using multiple sources of information is also possible (*http://www.cafasinontario. ca/html/about-about.asp*).

Child and Adolescent Service Intensity Instrument (CASII) (American Association of Community Psychiatrists 1999)

The American Association of Community Psychiatrists developed the CASII, formerly called CALOCUS, to measure the appropriate level of care for a youth that has come to the attention of a public agency. There are six dimensions (eight ratings) that are standardized. The ratings are quantified but also lie along a continuum. Three distinct types of disorders are used: psychiatric disorders, substance use disorders, and developmental disorders. A combined score is used to generate a level of care recommendation. For more information on the CASII, please email Kristin Kroeger Ptakowski at kkroeger@aacap. org (*http://www.aacap.org/clinical/CASII/*).

Child and Adolescent Risk Evaluation (CARE) (Seifert 2003)

The CARE assesses the need for structure and placement in a restrictive environment. It determines if a youth will need weekly outpatient, intensive outpatient, group home, or residential treatment. It is an easy tool to use for creating a multifaceted case management plan. Validity statistics are equivalent to CASII and CAFAS on most restrictive placement.

Comparison Risk Tools

The completion of the risk assessment tool first requires that the clinician gather a complete psychosocial history based on record review, direct interviews with the child or adolescent, and interviews with collateral informants such as parents, teachers, therapists, and social service agency workers (American Academy of Child and Adolescent Psychiatry; Rich 2003). Each risk tool has characteristics that are unique to that tool. By comparing tools, a practitioner can determine which tool(s) are best suited to their needs and their population(s). There are a variety of ways to compare tools; I use three sets of criteria to compare existing tools. The tools listed here are not exhaustive, but include those most commonly used by practitioners.

The SAVRY and the EARL-20 use guided clinical interviews. The factors included in the tools are based on pertinent literature in the field, including published studies. The PCL and the YLSI have empirically-based scoring systems and cut-off scores. The DVI is self-report and includes suggestions for treatment, as does the YLS/CMI.

There is professional debate about the use of actuarial tools and risk assessment with juveniles. Reasoning against guided clinical judgment without statistical validation is that we cannot guarantee the accuracy of our measures. The argument against risk tools that go beyond a guided clinical assessment and use scoring systems and cut-off scores similar to the adult risk tools are fears of labeling that does not change over time and the inability of existing tools to take into account the plasticity of youth development.

Violence is an interpersonal behavior that has a developmental trajectory, influenced by environment, caregiver bonding, neurological development, and child characteristics, such as temperament, genetics, and intelligence. A risk tool that measures dynamic factors that change over time as well as historical factors could capture a measure of risk at a particular point in time. The measure should present treatment options rather than just measuring risk.

It is also important to determine the appropriate level and type of services needed for all youth so that they may grow, mature, and be successful. There is a portion of the youthful population that has one or two minor problems that only need minimal services in one system and don't need to be overwhelmed by intervention from multiple agencies. There are also youth who are necessarily served by multiple public agencies (i.e. DSS, DJS, MHA, Education), have problems in more than one domain (psychiatric, legal, school, interpersonal), and need multiple services. Their families also may have numerous difficulties (e.g. abuse, violence, psychiatric problems, substance abuse) that need treatment.

According to the American Academy of Child and Adolescent Psychiatry American Association of Community Psychiatrists, "There have been a number of previous attempts to use assessments as a method of determining level of care needs in children and adolescents." This group found that it is important to look at what assessment tools and intervention models are supported by research. Their work was to develop an effective range of services based on the use of validated assessments of multiple areas of functioning. A cost-effective system of care should be based on a validated tool to determine the level and intensity of services needed. A reliable and valid case management tool is also needed to determine the type of services needed. If multiple agencies used the same tools, it might facilitate communication among agencies as well.

Several instruments have been developed in an attempt to meet these needs, such as the CAFAS, YLS/CMI, CARE, and CASII. All tools have acceptable reliability, a manual, and are peer-reviewed. The CAFAS, CASII, YLS/CMI, and CARE also indicate level or intensity of services needed.

Preliminary Study Comparing the PCL-YV, SAVRY, and the CARE as Violence Risk Assessment Tools

Files of 21 clients from an East Coast mental health facility were randomly chosen for the study (Seifert, unpublished manuscript 2004). All caregivers of minor clients signed a research-informed consent at the time of intake. All caregivers were informed that they had the right to not have their children participate in the study.

The PCL-YV (Forth, et al. 2003), CARE (Seifert 2003), and the SAVRY (Borum, et al. 2000) were administered by file review rather than by interview. There was one male and one female evaluator. Both had extensive experience with the risk tools. The identity of all participants was protected by using identification numbers rather than names.

While this is a very small sample, all three instruments were significantly associated with past and future assaults. In the instance of the CARE, the case management tool gives counselors guidance in what type of therapy to provide to an individual. The SAVRY, PCL-YV, and CARE are all significantly correlated with each other, indicating that they measure similar constructs (risk for violence). All three instruments were significantly associated with a variable that combined past violence and self-harm. Additionally, all of the instruments were significantly related to future assaultive behavior. When future aggression to others was combined with future aggression to self, all three instruments were significantly associated with this variable. This means that these tools measure aggression, whether to self or others. All of the instruments were significantly correlated with attachment problems, and attachment problems were significantly correlated with past and future violence. It appears that the CARE,

PCL-YV, and SAVRY can all be used to assess future violence effec-tively. However, while this was a promising start, more research is needed that compares these three tools.

Chapter 9

Assessment of Adult Risk of Violence and Sexual Offending

In one of the mental health segregation units in which I worked, a very smooth-talking, slick, psychopathic inmate had been writing wrathful letters about the devil and leaving them in places where the staff would find them. Officers brought Thomas to me to assess his risk of future dangerousness.

This guy made the hair on the back of my neck stand on end. Another mental health professional believed he was not dangerous, citing the facts that he was very bright and attended programming, and that there was no history of assaults within the prison. This colleague said, "He's not dangerous, he's just making noise, trying to stir things up and get attention." I disagreed.

I decided that my colleague's opinion was probably more accurate than my "hair-standing-on-end factor," so I acquiesced. After all, the other professional outranked me. Since that time I have heard others talk about such instinctual reactions as hair standing up and skin crawling as very good indicators of predators seeking prey. It must be how a mouse feels when it is being chased by a cat. I later regretted compromising my judgment, realizing it was a mistake on both my part and my colleague's to ignore my instinctual reaction.

All we had was clinical judgment at the time; this was before I had ever heard of an actuarial risk tool. Clinical judgment of future dangerousness is only slightly better than chance (Quinsey et. al., 1998). One of us thought the inmate was dangerous and one did not.

In a few days, officers brought Thomas back to me because of "strange" talk. I met with him in a large open area. A half a dozen correctional officers and as many nurses were in the general vicinity. As I began the standard interview, Thomas grabbed me.

"You bitch!" he screamed.

He pushed me against the cold, bare, grey wall with both hands. He was very strong, much more powerful than I. His cold, dark eyes seemed to burn a hole completely through me. I was terrified — and for one of the few times in my life speechless — as he took us all by surprise. As if from down a tunnel and far away, I heard one of the nurses yell, "Get him! Get him! For God's sake, somebody get him!"

Four officers grabbed him and wrestled him to the floor. They were joined by three more. They finally subdued Thomas enough to give him an injection and he stopped fighting. Dazed and shaken, I only remember parts of the incident and what others have told me about what happened.

As we all found out later, he was very capable of killing innocent people and wanted others to kill him. At his trial he said that he wanted to dig up his victims, grind them into a powder and feed them to their families. Several years later, Thomas was released from prison. Very shortly after his release, he killed three young people. When the police surrounded him before his capture, I was told it appeared as if he wanted the police to shoot him.

Thomas was severely abused and molested as both a child and a teenager. He never learned appropriate ways to interact with other human beings. How could he, given his history? This, again, is not to justify his actions, but merely to try to understand the roots so that we can improve prevention, assessment, and treatment procedures. The take-home conclusion here is that valid and reliable risk tools are a necessary weapon in our assessment arsenal. To know which one to use, we need to compare their characteristics and choose the one that is right for a certain population. Had Thomas been given the RME (Risk Management Evaluation, Seifert 2006), his score would have been 36 — high risk for future assaults. At that time in my career, I neither knew the questions to ask to determine dangerousness, nor the interventions needed to prevent future dangerousness. My question to you is, knowing what we now know about one of the developmental paths of interpersonal violence, can we prevent future Thomases from taking the all-too-predictable path of violence through life? If we use validated risk tools, can we prevent dangerous criminals from being released from jail or sent on home visits from the forensic hospital too early?

Descriptions of the Various Adult Violence Risk Tools

Why is it important to talk about adult risk assessment and management in the context of prevention, assessment, and treatment of youth violence? Children who have been abused and exposed to domestic violence are at risk for violence to self and others. They often come from violent families. When these families come to the attention of the courts or mental health or child welfare agencies, it is important to assess the risk that violent parents pose to their children, and to manage that risk. This will prevent or ameliorate the influence of family violence on children. We must, as a society, step in when children are abused or exposed to violence, to ensure that they get counseling and moved to a more positive environment in order to protect both the children and any people who might have ended up on the receiving end of their violence. Since the prediction of adult dangerousness using clinical judgment alone is also only slightly better than chance, these agencies should begin to use actuarial tools, as Canadian agencies do routinely.

Level of Service Inventory (LSI-R) (Andrews and Bonta 1995, 1998)

The Level of Service Inventory uses 54 risk items to assess the level of structure and supervision that an offender might need. The LSI-R (Andrews and Bonta 1995, 1998) is one of the most widely used measures of general criminal recidivism (Gendreau et al. 1996). The LSI-R has the important advantage of including a substantial number of dynamic factors. It provides guidance in terms of level of structure or security needed by an adult male or female offender. Evaluations of sexual offenders, however, should not rely exclusively on the LSI-R, since it does not include items specifically related to sexual recidivism (e.g., relationship to victims) (Hanson 2000).

Historical, Clinical, Risk — 20 (HCR-20) (Webster et al. 1997)

The HCR-20 is intended for use with civil psychiatric, forensic, and criminal justice populations. It is a checklist of 20 risk factors for violent behavior. The items cover historical, clinical, and risk management issues. One item is the PCL-R score.

The Violence Risk Appraisal Guide (VRAG) (Quinsey et al. 1998)

The VRAG is an accurate risk measure for general violence, but it was not intended to assess the risk for sexual recidivism. It is a 12-item scale, which includes the PCL-R score. It was validated on adult mentally-disordered offenders.

Domestic Violence Inventory (DVI) (Behavior Data Systems, Ltd. 1996)

DVI is an instrument for evaluating clients who have been accused or convicted of domestic violence. Scales include Truthfulness, Alcohol and Drug, Violence (Lethality), Control, and Stress Coping. It is a self-report instrument with all of the problems associated with self-report. The DVI is correlated with the PD scale of the MMPI and domestic violent offending.

Violence Eliciting Situation Inventory (VESI) (Nussbaum, unpublished manuscript)

The VESI is based on experimental animal aggression literature. The client is asked to provide four situations in each of these categories: situation would a) Definitely make them violent, b) Possibly make them violent, or c) Irritate them, but not make them violent. A new version of this tool is being developed. The VESI score is significantly correlated (r = .58) with violence density (frequency and severity). Because offenders may try to disguise their predatory attitudes on self-report measures, the VESI provides a less-transparent way of assessing violent propensity.

Violence Risk Assessment Scale (VRS) (Wong and Gordon 1996)

The VRS has 6 static and 23 dynamic factors used to assess the risk of future violence by incarcerated offenders.

Spousal Assault Risk Assessment Guide (SARA) (Kropp et al. 1999)

The SARA is a 20-item set of risk factors for use in the assessment of spousal assault. The items are based on a review of the literature on spousal abuse. The SARA was designed as a means for gathering comprehensive data about risk in domestic violence cases.

Risk Management Evaluation — Male and Female (RME) (Seifert 2002)

The RME is a risk instrument based on a biopsychosocial-ecological theory of violence (Seifert 2003). Human behavior is the result of the interaction of a person's physical and social environment, and his or her physical, psychological, and developmental make-up. Each person is a unique composition of personal and environmental vulnerabilities and resiliencies. When the number of risks is great and the resiliencies are few, this balance reaches a threshold, and the likelihood of violence increases. However, not all factors have the same impact on behavior; therefore, items of a risk instrument should have different weights. It is not sufficient to measure the risk of future violence. It is necessary to describe intervention strategies as well. Unlike existing risk tools, the RME is such an instrument.

The RME contains clinical items, dynamic factors, resiliency factors, and risk management plans. Dynamic risk factors can measure changes in skills that may help reduce recidivism and static factors are items that do not change, such as an abuse history. The RME tools include the Adult RME for males, RME for females, RME female screening tool, and the RME for sexual offenders (Seifert, in press).

Assessments of risk for violence should evaluate all possible problem areas, including past behavior, community, family, peer, job/school, neurological, and mental health. The RME is a violence risk evaluation for adult males and females; the sample includes 162 males, 128 females, and 60 sexual offenders in an outpatient/forensic mental health setting. Standardization using a prison sample is underway. Studies have found that the risk factors for adult violence are similar or the same as the risk factors for youth violence. Consequently, the RME uses the same items as the youth version, but after further research and analysis the items have been re-worded and item weights have been changed to be appropriate for and consistent with the adult sample (Seifert 2002). Higher rates of violent recidivism and other offending behaviors are found when there are greater numbers of risk factors and fewer resiliency factors.

Risk categories include:

- Individual characteristics such as history of violence, poor anger management, psychosis, and harming animals
- Peer interactions like bullying behaviors and deviant peer group
- Work, school, and educational problems, such as a lack of work success
- Family characteristics such as exposure to violence during childhood and a history of harsh disciplinary practices by parents

Work success, positive activities, and pro-social and achievable future goals are examples of resiliency factors.

A regression analysis of the sample showed that the strongest predictor of adult assault history was any past aggression, attachment problems, family history of substance abuse or psychiatric problems, or one or both parents addicted, dead, or uninvolved in the adult's life as a child. There was one protective factor in the past assault analysis. It was appropriate discipline in childhood (R =.93, F = 6.72, p = .00). The strongest significant predictors of chronic assaults were: past aggression that is not chronic, use of a weapon, caregivers used inappropriate discipline when adult was a child, and severity of behavior problem history (r = .88, F = 6.86, p = .00). There is a regression analysis of severe assaults (those that cause harm requiring medical care for the victim). Other factors are: non-severe assaults, use of a weapon, escape from custody, disappearance for days at a time, runaway behavior as a child, belief in the legitimacy of aggression as a means to an end, psychiatric problems, deviant peers, low family warmth, and high conflict as a child or adult (R =.88, F = 3.57, p = .00).

The correlation between RME score and assault history is .66 (p = .00). The correlation with future aggression on a sub-sample of 32 clients is .61 (p = .00). The correlation of the RME total score with a history of behavior problems is .68 (p = .00).

Assessment of Risk of Adult Sexual Offending

Ted Bundy sexually assaulted at least some of his murder victims. His history is described in Chapter 3. He engaged in voyeurism as a youth and was reportedly fascinated with images of sex and violence. I will examine his case with some of the assessments described below.

The Sex Offender Risk Appraisal Guide (SORAG) (Quinsey et al. 1998)

The SORAG is revision of the VRAG for sexual offenders. The resulting scale is a moderate predictor of general violent recidivism and sexual recidivism. There are 14 items based on the VRAG. One item is the PCL-R score.

Minnesota Sex Offender Screening Tool (MnSOST) (Epperson, Kaul, and Huot 1995; Epperson, Kaul, and Hasselton 1998)

The MnSOST was specifically designed to assess the risk of violent and sexual recidivism among extra-familial child molesters and rapists (incest offenders are excluded). It had 16 static and dynamic factors. The MnSOST-R uses the same items as the original version, but uses an empirically-based weighting system. The empirical weights increase the predictive accuracy of the scale but have yet to be cross-validated on a new sample.

Static-99 (Hanson and Thornton 1999)

The Static-99 combined the RRASOR items with some items from Thornton's Structured Anchored Clinical Judgment scale (SAC-J; Grubin 1998). When tested in four diverse samples, the resulting scale predicted sexual offense recidivism (average r = .33) better than either original scale (RRASOR or SAC-J). Static-99 also shows at least moderate accuracy in predicting any violent recidivism (average r = .32). A new version is in the developmental stages.

The Rapid Risk Assessment for Sexual Offense Recidivism (RRASOR) (Hanson 1997)

The RRASOR was developed to assess the risk for sexual offense recidivism using four easily-scored static items. The initial pool of items was selected from Hanson and Bussière's (1998) meta-analysis. It was tested on seven samples from Canada, the U.S., and the UK. The scale is moderately accurate in the prediction of sexual recidivism. The standardization pool is primarily a forensic population.

Sex Offender Needs Assessment (SONAR) (Hanson and Harris 2000)

This 9-item scale is used to measure change in risk level of sex offenders. It includes 5 stable factors and 4 acute factors.

Sexual Violence Risk (SVR-20) (Boer et al. 1997)

The SVR-20 is a 20-item guide for assessing violence risk in sex offenders. Little was found on its psychometrics.

Risk Management Evaluation — Sexual Offenders (RME-SO) (Seifert, unpublished manuscript)

The RME-SO is based on the same premises and items as the RME for males and females. Retrospective and prospective studies have been carried out (unpublished). Reliability and validity are good.

Sexual Adjustment Scale (SAI) (Behavior Data Systems)

The SAI is a self-report inventory of sexual behaviors. Once scored, the report includes a risk management section. Psychometrics on this scale have not been found in the literature. It has all the problems associated with self-report measures and this population.

Assessment of Risk for Future Adult Sexual Offending

Barbaree et al. (2001) found that when assessing 215 sex offenders who had been out of prison an average of 4.5 years, the Violence Risk Appraisal Guide, Sex Offender Risk Appraisal Guide, Rapid Risk Assessment of Sexual Offense Recidivism, and Static-99 predicted general recidivism, serious (violent and sexual) recidivism, and sexual recidivism in a valid manner. However, The Minnesota Sex Offender Screening Tool-Revised and the Multifactorial Assessment of Sex Offender Risk for Recidivism predicted general recidivism, but did not significantly predict serious or sexual recidivism, while the Psychopathy Checklist-Revised predicted general and serious recidivism but not sexual recidivism.

Using Ted Bundy as our example, I have scored him on the RRASOR, Static-99, and RME-SO. At the time of his trial, Bundy had a score of four on the RRASOR. This gives him a 33% chance of recidivism for a sexual offense at 5 years and 49 percent at 10 years. He did escape while awaiting trial and claimed five more victims, but through my research, I am unclear if any of these victims were sexually as well as physically assaulted. On the Static-99 (there is a newer version now being evaluated), Bundy received a score of five, or a medium-high risk for future sexual offending. On the RME-SO, he has a score of 27, placing him in the high risk range for sexual re-offense. Additionally, a high level of structure is recommended from the results.

At the end of his trial, had he not been executed, Ted Bundy was at medium-high risk of future sexual offending and high risk for future violence. He therefore would have needed to be placed in a high level of security. While Bundy may not have been dangerous to male inmates, he would have posed a risk to female staff and appropriate precautions would have needed to be taken. I offer as an example that in several recent cases, offenders followed female counselors to their offices and raped them. Consequently, these tools are needed to determine the level of risk these inmates pose to staff and other inmates, as well as to the general public upon their release.

The Importance of a Methodical Approach to Assessment

Assessment of risk of future violent or sexual dangerousness to self or others must be approached methodically. After all, risk assessment is an emerging field and many tools are in the developmental or research stages. It is likely that several tools will be used simultaneously, because each uses a slightly different risk perspective and may provide unique information. Comparing tools allows a practitioner to choose the tool that best suits his population and situation. Most of the traditional risk tools do not include case or risk management tools. Older tools have more peer review and cross validation studies than newer tools. However, some of the newer tools are showing stronger construct and predictive validity than some of the older tools.

Assessment Limitations

Research articles on the relationships between violence, childhood trauma, and attachment disorders are still very limited. Our understanding of the roots, nature, and treatment of violence is in its infancy. Only a few provide therapy for attachment disorders. Those providing therapy are often not researchers. Levy and Orlans, James, Cline, Welch, Levine, and Shapiro are providing various approaches to attachment and trauma therapy. Levy (1998) reports that 80 percent of the child welfare population is attachment-disordered and that boys with attachment problems are three times more likely to be violent. Yet these child welfare agencies are not often on the leading edge of therapeutic technology or theory. The few therapists who are doing this work cannot begin to meet the need. More research and treatment money is needed, as well as a commitment to meet the needs of abused and neglected children and those exposed to domestic violence.

In Part III, we will take a step beyond assessment, moving on to actual treatment methods for children with DAP and other youths at a high risk for violence. Like assessments, since research is still evolving in the fields of violence and mental health, many treatments are hopeful, yet not entirely proven.

Part 3

Treatment

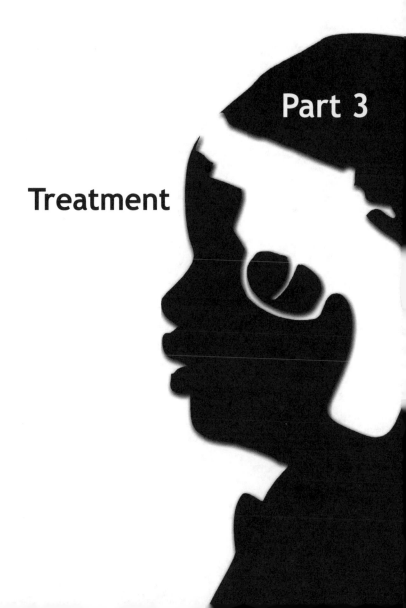

Chapter 10

Treatment for Children with Disrupted Attachment Patterns

Treatment for attachment problems is still in the developmental stages. However, increased focus on study in this area is essential in order to develop methods for preventing children from developing inappropriate interpersonal behaviors and skills. Because of the controversy and the lack of research, the conservative approach would be to use established therapies with a proven track record and add what is known about Disrupted Attachment Patterns and their treatment with training and supervision. One must be informed about all sides of the debate on attachment theory, assessment, and treatment. Attachment therapies are basically about resolving trauma, building skills, fostering attachments and appropriate relationships, and relationship skills. Individual therapy alone is not sufficient. Family therapy (even with a substitute family) must be part of the work. Part III attempts to put treatment into perspective.

There are models for treatment of attachment disorders developed by Foster Cline (1979), Terry Levy and Michael Orlans (1998), Martha Welch (1989), and Beverly James (1994). Foster Cline developed Rage Reduction Therapy with the idea that it was necessary to tap into the pre-verbal emotional state in order to treat attachment disorders. He used a format to get the child to identify areas that needed to be changed, to commit to the work and work hard, and to do it his (the therapist's) way. He then attempted to tap into strong emotional states and help the child work them through.

Levy and Orlans developed a two-week intensive in Colorado, followed by long-term therapy by the hometown therapist. The Levy and Orlans model uses a holding type therapy, psychodrama, cognitive restructuring, healing the inner child, and nurturing and re-parenting in a family therapy format.

Martha Welch wrote a book called *Holding Time,* which included holding a child every day, even if against her will. This is to break down the barriers preventing attachment from taking place. There is very strong controversy surrounding this technique, however, due to suggestions that holding therapies using coercive techniques are abusive and should not be used.

There have been strong objections to the holding, rebirthing, and rage reduction therapies, especially since these practices caused the deaths of several children. For instance, in Colorado in 2000, Candace Newmaker died during a rebirthing therapy, which was meant to recreate the birthing process in order to help her bond with her mother. The blankets from which she was to emerge were held too tightly and she died trying to free herself. Rebirthing therapy has therefore been banned in Colorado. Consequently, one needs to be very cautious, if not avoid, coercive holding therapies until there is more research to demonstrate what works and what does not — and, of course, what is safe — in these cases. In my mind, it is just not

worth the chance that harm would come to a child, even acciden-
tally. Each person must make that choice for themselves. Another
precaution is for the therapists to clearly and carefully word their
instructions so they are not mistaken or misused by caregivers. Caregivers who use shaming techniques, such as having the child wear
soiled underwear on his head or a boy wearing a dress to school when
he doesn't want to, are unacceptable. Good common sense should
prevail in these cases.

More research is also certainly needed. Beverly James (1994) created and taught a long-term therapy model. She brings together the
concepts of attachment, trauma, and development to guide the interventions with children with disrupted attachment problems. Daniel
Hughes, in *Facilitating Developmental Attachment* (2003), discusses a
theory of conflict and resolution as one of the curative factors in attachment therapy. For Hughes, the development of interpersonal skills
comes from working through everyday situations, including conflict and
discipline, to create a resolution and bonding with loved ones. This is
very much oversimplified, but I highly recommend his book.

Information about the existing theories, assessments, and therapies
relating to attachment can be found at the following websites:

- Attachment Disorder Assessment Scale for Children:
  http://www.sswr.org/papers2001/420.htm
- Attach Organization: *http://www.Attach.org/*
- Evergreen Consultants, Terry Levy and Michael Orlans:
  http://attachmenttherapy.com/

The holistic/developmental model presented here incorporates ideas from these and other existing models. What the theories have in common are a set of principles based on the needs of the child that guide the work. However, keep in mind that more useful research of a therapy with a strong theoretical base is still needed.

A holistic/developmentally-based treatment for the dysfunction in the child/caregiver bond has five parts. Some of the topics are:

- Family work
- Commitment to the work
- Identifying and processing the trauma
- Re-examining and restructuring the patterns of thinking, feeling, and behaving that have resulted
- Empowerment of the client to break free from the damage caused by abuse and neglect
- Bilateral stimulation with sensory integration

Also important is coordination of care by other providers through a treatment team that addresses specific areas of dysfunction, such as school or the juvenile justice system, including the youth and family. The holistic model is based on the premise that attachment difficulties affect several aspects of a child's development and, as such, all disturbances in functioning must be treated. It is not sufficient to work only with the child. The caregivers must be involved in the therapy and they must have a level of maturity that makes it possible for them to provide structure, limits, and nurturing without being excessively punitive.

Additionally, when a child's school and community functioning has been affected, there should be appropriate interventions in those

arenas, as well. The therapy needs to address difficulties with problem-solving, learning, self-soothing, self-harm, anger management,
communicating feelings, misperceptions, depression, anxiety, eating
disorders, and social skills.

The techniques of this treatment are didactic, physical, and psychotherapeutic, and have several theoretical underpinnings. Attachment
therapy derives from many theories, including Neurolinguistic Programming, psychodynamic theory, Gestalt, psychodrama, family
systems, as well as cognitive and existing attachment therapies.
A combination of individual and group work can be used quite effectively. Because attachment is basic to human functioning, and
is formed pre-verbally, therapy must involve some physical activity
that accesses the pre-verbal areas of the brain and memory. This
is done in part by psychodrama, dance, drumming, movement, and
art. These activities can facilitate appropriate emotional development because using creativity helps the child heal from trauma. It is
important to provide explanation of the process to participants as the
work progresses.

There are several concepts that have been developed by different
practitioners that can be useful in helping a child understand the development of his disorder and his reaction to it. This understanding
then empowers the child to make changes that improve the quality of
his life. In the rest of this chapter I will cover several specific treatment options.

Attachment Informed Therapy

It is not necessary to be an "expert" in attachment therapy to work
with children with Disrupted Attachment Patterns. Many "traditional

therapies" are useful, especially for children who have attachment problems rather than a severe disorder. However, it is necessary to be informed about the theory, concepts, and available alternatives for therapy. It is also important for therapists to be very aware of their limitations, and to use supervision and consultation often in this work. I recommend this precaution not only for the quality of the work, but also for the strain that such complex cases can place on the therapist's psyche and energy level.

Affective Attunement

It is hypothesized that affective attunement with the primary caregiver was disrupted or not achieved for children with negative bonding experiences. Therefore treatment will involve events that help the child feel emotionally "in tune" with the caregivers. For instance, in psychodrama, when the end of the story is changed to one of empowerment, it is important for the caregivers as well as the child to be involved in the change so that they can feel relief and re-laxation at the same time as the child. Activities that allow the child to feel understood by the caregivers are important.

Rapport Building

As with all good therapies, one must start with establishing rapport. This is done through reflective listening, mirroring, and entrainment. By mirroring and reflecting back the verbal and body language and actions of the client, the child can begin to feel safe and understood. It is imperative that the therapists create safe containment within the therapy session. This means that strong emotions can be expressed in a safe place and not get out of the control of the therapist.

Commitment to the Work

Milton, Erickson, Cline, Levy, and others use techniques designed to elicit commitment to the work. Erickson in particular established that it is important to start where the client is. Thus therapy begins by having the client make a "grocery list" of behaviors or situations that the client wants to work on changing. This allows the therapy to be a reciprocal process in which the client expresses a commitment to change elements of his life that he has chosen. The therapy can be difficult and painful, and commitment helps the client to keep going.

For example, a child's goal could be, *I would like my mother to not yell at me so much.* The therapist and parents (pre-prompted) elaborately exclaim what a great goal that is and everyone, including the child, commits to that goal. The therapist then asks the parents to name one of their goals. She could say, *Now just to be fair, we should ask your parents to name a goal, too.* The same process repeats as the parents exclaim what a good goal it is and the therapist attempts to get commitment from everyone to the goal. As great as this sounds, however, it sometimes backfires. The child may refuse to support the parental goals. One way to fix this is to say to the child, *You are very right. I think you should speak your mind and tell your mother and father how you feel about this goal and why.* (It is important that no matter what the child says, you find a way to reframe it as cooperation and reinforce it because that is ultimately your goal. Reinforcement will gain you more than a struggle will.) You can then set up a conversation within the family using the traditional dialogue:

Child: I feel ____ when you ____ because ____.
Parent: What I heard you say is ____. Did I get it right?

Child: Yes. or Yes, but _____.

Parent: I feel _____ when you _____, because _____.

If the child still refuses to participate then the therapist says, *You are exactly right, I don't want you to speak for yourself. I will speak for you.* The therapist speaks for the child. Sometimes the child will interrupt and say that's not right and take his own part. Sometimes he won't. Either way, you did not get into a will struggle and you modeled appropriate reciprocity for the child. Never nag a child to join in. Just say that that is really what you wanted him to do after all. What you're doing is a subtle form of always getting compliance out of the child no matter what he does or says.

Prescribing the Symptom

Prescribing the Symptom can be found in the work of Victor Frankel and Jay Haley. It is a method that feels counterintuitive, is sometimes scary, and must be used carefully and judiciously. Since youth with DAP are primarily oppositional, you tell them to do the opposite of what you really want them to do and give it a schedule and prescribed way to do it. For instance, the child always leaves his clothes in the middle of the bathroom floor. You tell the child that he is to continue to do that, but must not forget to do so — you want to see how high the pile can get because you once knew someone who filled an entire bathroom with clothes. *Of course it was inconvenient because the clothes had to stay there, and he had nothing to wear, but who cares.*

Children often see the silliness of this right away. This is good, because you want a child to see that it is silly. You let the child try it for one week and report the results to you the next week. If he picks up his clothes, then you praise him for doing what you wanted him to do after all. If he leaves his clothes in the bathroom, then praise him for following your directions. Either way, he has complied and gotten praise. The natural consequences are that the behavior becomes inconvenient and **the child decides he wants to change that behavior.** Mom, this is important: Don't clean it up for him!

The reason why it is important to have very stable caregivers is that this type of technique is a slippery slope. Unstable parents can take things to extremes. One mother sent her child to school dressed in his sister's clothes and another sent the child to school with urine filled underpants on his head as a punishment. Obviously this goes too far and is abusive. Therapists will have to carefully monitor these techniques and their effects on the child and family.

Cognitive Techniques for Social Skills, Anger Management, and Thinking Errors

Because abused and neglected children learn very early to suppress feelings in self-protection, they must acquire appropriate methods of understanding and communicating feelings. A very young child may say, *I hate you* or *I wish you were dead* instead of, *I'm very angry with you.* He may act out anger physically with tantrums, hitting others, or self-harm because he does not have the words to express feelings or the ability to self-soothe. He may need to learn anger management and self-soothing techniques, which can be taught using cognitive/behavioral methods. There are many pre-programmed exercises available on the market, many of which are appropriate for group work. Since attachment-disordered children usually have weak problem-solving skills as well, they must learn to reason, generate alternatives, and weigh consequences of potential actions.

Loss Cycle

Another important concept to help a child understand his own behavior, thoughts, feelings, and attitudes is the Loss Cycle. There are several models based on the original work by Elizabeth Kubler-Ross (Ross and Kessler 2005). Abuse and neglect involve a loss of parental love and nurturing. All children instinctively know that they need this nurturing. The stages of loss are no different than what is experienced from the death of a loved one. The child experiences confusion, denial, bargaining, anger, and deep sadness. It is important for the therapist to help him proceed to the next steps in the loss cycle, such as skills gained or lessons learned, acceptance, and integration.

It looks like this:

Figure 10.1 – The Loss Cycle (Kubler and Ross)

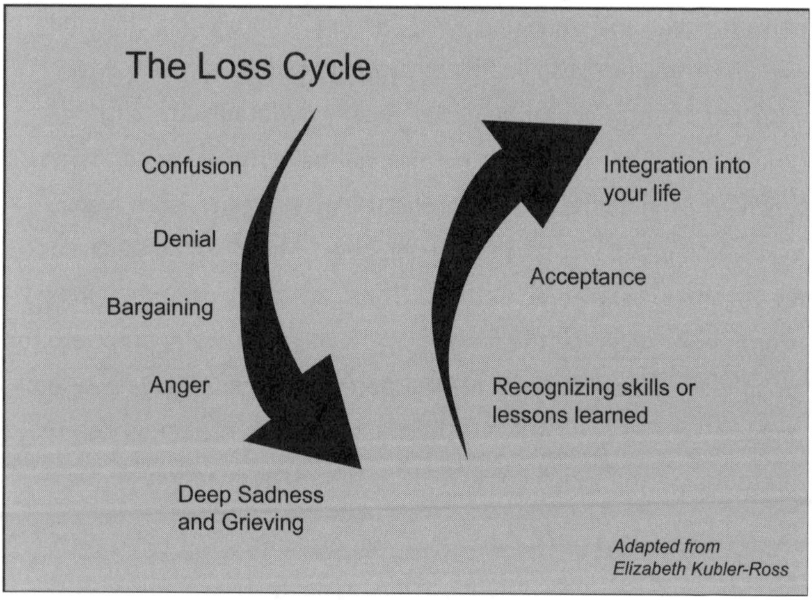

The Loss Cycle

Confusion

Denial

Bargaining

Anger

Deep Sadness
and Grieving

Integration into
your life

Acceptance

Recognizing skills or
lessons learned

*Adapted from
Elizabeth Kubler-Ross*

First Year Cycle of Life

Levy and Orlans (1998) developed techniques for the First Year Cycle of Life as part of their two-week intensive therapy. They ask a sequence of questions to help clients identify and understand the source of their rage, such as:

> **Therapist:** What do all babies need?
>
> **Child:** Love, food, safety.
>
> **Therapist:** How do babies let others know what they need?
>
> **Child:** Cry, yell.
>
> **Therapist:** What do you think happens when the baby's needs are met?
>
> **Child:** He is happy.
>
> **Therapist:** What do you think happens when the baby's needs are not met?
>
> **Child:** He is sad or angry.
>
> **Therapist:** How do you think you felt when you were a baby and your needs were not met?
>
> **Child:** I must have felt sad or angry.

It is explained that when infants have their needs met and are well taken care of, they feel relieved, relaxed, and trusting. When they are abused or neglected, they feel rage and self-loathing, and they trust no one. They become their own "boss." They say to themselves, *I can't trust "big people" or anyone else. No one will ever be the boss of me.* For the first time, these children and adolescents have the opportunity to understand the source of the rage they feel inside and their extreme lack of trust. Since these feeling states are pre-verbal, this exercise gives them a language to express what they feel. After accessing some early memories, Dr. Levy uses exercises in which the child kicks in a scissors-like fashion while being held. Some traumatic memories may be state-dependent and need a level of arousal to access them. Kicking and shouting can elicit physiological arousal. I recommend having the caregivers do the holding and to not use coercive techniques that may re-traumatize the child.

Bilateral Physical Stimulation

Eye Movement Desensitization Reprocessing (EMDR), created by Francine Shapiro (1997), has been used to process traumatic memories. It involves bilateral stimulation and shows great promise for the treatment of trauma. It is believed that the bilateral processing of sensation and emotion may be a very important part of attachment therapy. One theory is that thoughts, feelings, and sensations of significant trauma can be locked in the brain, unprocessed, continually replayed like a never-ending film loop. EMDR reprocesses the negative emotions associated with these events, allowing the psyche to proceed to a healthier state of well-being. Some recent studies indicate that it is the desensitization or exposure part of the therapy that is the most effective part of the process. Levy and Orlans (1998) have the child kick in scissors fashion while being held on the lap to activate the areas of the brain that govern kinesis and to generate arousal that simulates an infant need state. It may also function to induce a hypnotic regression to access pre-verbal memories. It is also a type of bilateral stimulation that may have effects similar to EMDR. Peter Levine has also written about the physical processing of trauma (1997).

Nurturing Touch

Nurturing physical touch is necessary for all human well-being. Children with DAP have been deprived of loving touch. Their recovery will involve some level or type of nurturing physical contact with another person. Some believe that trust and deep emotional connection are accomplished by holding the child as one would an infant, looking into his eyes, and establishing the requirement for honesty between client and therapist (Levy and Orlans 1998; Welch 1989). Physical proximity, eye contact, and honesty are very difficult for the attachment-disordered child. It takes constant gentle encouragement to help the client make new, healthier patterns of relating. Lack of trust, reciprocity, and emotional connection are the core of the disorder, and establishing them is the heart of the recovery. This must be done physically as well as emotionally.

Levy, Orlans (1998), and Welch (1989) use a "holding" technique in their therapy. This technique, because it is both unique and controversial, must be done carefully; I recommend using observers and videotaping sessions. Levy and Orlans use physical closeness that simulates the parent/infant bond to access the pre-verbal part of the psyche. It may also induce a hypnotic regression to an infant state. This is done with eye contact and holding the child on your lap and in your arms while sitting, much in the way you would an infant. This is an important part of the therapy because of the need for nurturing touch. While many therapists do not use therapist holding techniques, some still find it to be an important component. Some in the field are moving toward more non-coercive nurturing, holding and touch by caregivers instead of therapists. It remains a controversial area and not one to be taken lightly. Be well-informed and use supervision and training before choosing techniques to use.

Relaxation Exercises and Visualization
The use of relaxation exercises, deep breathing, visualization,

counting breaths, and deep muscle relaxation can be used to reduce anxiety and fearfulness, and increase coping between sessions. I like the "7-7-7" method. The 7-7-7 method starts with breathing in deeply to the slow count of seven. Then, the child holds his breath to the count of seven and breathes out slowly to the count of seven. Instruct the child to expand the belly when doing this. Use self-talk to relax the muscle groups and to visualize a safe place.

By using "anchoring," the client can go to the safe place any time he needs to. Anchoring involves making a physical association like touching your knee while relaxing. With practice, touching the knee can become a trigger to access the relaxation response. Some thought and feeling patterns and memories may be sub-conscious and pre-verbal; it will take this state of relaxation to access them. Relaxation techniques are important skills to acquire. Teaching relaxation skills before the first discussion of trauma events is essential because children with DAP often lack the ability to self-sooth. They must have a way to manage emotions during the processing of trauma. Many relaxation CDs are available for purchase. My guided imagery relaxation CDs are available for purchase at *www.DrKathySeifert.com*.

Strong Sitting

Strong sitting is a technique used by Levy, Orlans, and others. It is a type of time-out where the child sits up straight, quietly and cross-legged on the floor at a particular designated spot. When I use this treatment method, I encourage thinking about what happened, looking inside for answers, deep breathing, and relaxation. Don't make it too long and make the time/age appropriate. Giving choices is also good — *You can do a half hour of sloppy sitting or fifteen minutes of strong sitting. It's your choice.* Remember, stay out of will struggles and pick your battles. Time-out guidelines use one minute per year of age of the child.

Psychodrama

We can help the client regain his power by getting rid of the past abuser or neglectful caregiver and standing up to him or her in psychodrama. It is important to re-enact little traumas first so that the child can build up to larger ones while learning to manage emotions and build coping skills. He can explore his own and others' thinking, feeling, and behaving, and be empowered to act by asking for help from the therapist or present caregiver. The client can shout at the abuser to get out of his life, mind, and dreams. By yelling with some energy, they can generate arousal and relief, as in the first year cycle of life. At that time, the heart is open for emotional connection to others. It is then important to rewrite the story, bringing it to a different, positive conclusion, where the abuse or neglect is ended and the child is appropriately cared for by the present caregiver. The template for positive and trusting relationships will still need work, but the child will be open to it. The connection can then be made to the present caregiver or therapist. From this, empathy and trust can be developed. Moral development can proceed with an understanding of reciprocity and balancing the greatest good for the group and the desires of the self.

Chain of Strength Memories

Every person has skills and things they do well. Have the youth establish a chain of strengths or skills that he uses to solve problems. In what situations has he been successfu? Re-enact situations of strong efficacy when the feeling is greatest; anchor it to a physical action like touching one's knee or cheek or a peace sign. To access the feeling, he only needs to use the anchor. Each time he uses or recognizes the chain, it is strengthened. This technique is probably best used with teens; because of its nature, it may be beyond the grasp of younger children. Always use the Chain of Strength before the Chain of Trauma Memories.

Chain of Trauma Memories

Children with DAP have generally had multiple traumas. The traumas are linked together in memory like a chain by their similarities. When a child faces a new situation with similar characteristics, he can react as if it is part of the chain of trauma. All of the old feelings ride up the chain as if they belong to today. In the therapy, one can pair the chain of traumas with the chain of strengths or skills. Then the youth can separate the feelings that belong to today from those that belong to a time in the past. I use, *That was then and this is now.* I actually have the child move with me across the room indicating the two places where we re-enacted old trauma and today's safety. I may repeat it several times. *That was then.* Walk across the room. *This is now.*

There is often the fear that the strong emotions associated with childhood trauma cannot be tolerated, or that one will explode in an uncontrollable fit of rage and terror once it is released. One of the tasks, then, is demonstrating that these emotions can be tolerated, understood, expressed, and overcome. Consequently, the client must experience the fear, sadness, and anger. This is done through a reenactment of the trauma with the resulting abreaction, which can be a very disquieting experience for both the youth and the therapist. The young person draws from the therapist's strength to help him work through his trauma. The therapist must learn to be very strong to help walk him through it, while the present caregivers help the child soothe himself when it is over. Soothing is important, since it is a weak or unlearned skill. Does this mean you scare the child to death? No, but you must show him he can tolerate and manage strong emotions. Again the therapist _must be_ thoroughly trained, seasoned, and skillful, and must always use supervision. It is too easy to get off track with such strong emotions. You must not push, but create that safe container where a child can experience his feelings in front of you and his caregivers.

Pain Avoidance Cycle

The Pain Avoidance Cycle involves avoiding emotional pain by act-ing out behaviorally instead of effectively communicating emotions. The work of Way and Balthazor (1990) with juvenile sex offenders uses a model for a pain avoidance cycle to help youngsters create a relapse prevention plan. I have found this model useful for helping attachment-disordered youths understand their acting-out cycle. An abused and neglected child needs techniques to help him cope with the tremendous pain associated with lack of parental love and atten-tion. The child has already learned to suppress tremendous emotional pain. This usually involves an avoidance activity or dissociation ac-complished by distancing himself emotionally from others. Cognitive distortions make it possible to justify "misbehavior" without concern for the well-being of self or others. Helping a child to describe his own acting-out cycle using this model can then help him understand his own behavior.

Figure 10.2 — The Acting-Out Cycle

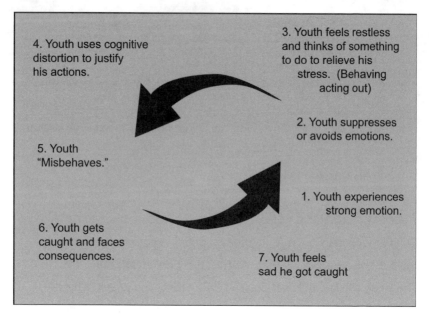

Rewriting the Child's Story

It has been said that the brain does not know the difference between reality and fantasy. As of yet, we have no evidence of this. However, if a youth can tell and then "rewrite" his "story," he can begin to have a new perspective on his life, himself, and his relationship with others. The new perspective can then become part of his reality. The child or teen often has the view that the abuser/neglectful parent was and is powerful, and he (the child) was and is weak, afraid, and defenseless. By rewriting his story, these associations can be changed so that violence becomes associated with weakness and poor choices. As the child/teen learns self-efficacy and self-control, he can create a positive image of strength for himself. The brain can then accept the new definitions of power and violence. Social reciprocity then can be added to the repertoire of personal skills.

I worked with a young boy, Shawn, whose mother was a drug addict who did not feed or care for him as she should. He had also been sexually molested at a very young age. This handsome little boy had then been adopted by wonderful parents at about age six. He had problems with lying, stealing, hording food, roaming the house at night, friendships with antisocial peers who often got into trouble, rages that ended in aggression, and sexual misconduct. In order to deal with the trauma he experienced with his birth mother, we re-enacted what we thought it was like for him in his mother's house. His "new (adopted) parents" watched the scene. I played the part of his "old" mother by disguising myself. I lounged on my chair and pretended to be happy and high. I did not respond to his cries for food or help. He had been prompted that if his "old mother" did not help him, he should call for someone who could help if the same scene happened today. (I am careful not to re-traumatize, but to emphasize the new "rewritten" scene.) Shawn called for his "new parents" to help him. They came quickly to the rescue and took care of his needs. They also made the "old mother" leave the room. Everyone, including the child, shouted for her not to come back. I see this as an empowerment stance while accepting assistance from "new parents."

Emotionally Stable Caregivers

The involvement of emotionally stable caregivers in the therapy cannot be over-emphasized. The general success of the therapy depends on it. They need to be educated about setting strong limits in a matter-of-fact way. They need to be a role model and teach the child how to be reciprocal. Nurturing is also an important factor. These children *need* yet *reject* love and a nurturing touch. It's difficult to continue to approach them in a loving manner due to their protests and rejections. If parents take this rejection personally and respond in anger, then it will interfere with bonding unless strongly balanced with nurturing. Strong anger can lead to abuse, which will prevent bonding from taking place. For the child it is trauma repetition, which is compulsive until mastered. A parent can feel anger rising and may be tempted to spank or hit the child. This is totally counter-productive for these children.

Love and Hurting Have Become "Hooked Together"

For children with Disrupted Attachment Patterns, love and hurt have been so closely associated that they come to believe that they cannot have one without the other. Learning how they came to be "hooked together" and helping to separate them can be a daunting task. The association is often made pre-verbally, and simply using words will not be sufficient to separate them. The therapist can help the child under-stand these concepts through her actions and attitudes. She is always there, never exploding, never abusive, always caring and nurturing, no matter how much the child acts out. This is why, when substitute caregivers are used, they must be carefully selected. These children can try anyone's patience severely. If there are abusive tendencies or anger-control problems in the caregiver, these children will draw them out. It is only with the absence of abuse, regardless of their behavior, that they can make new associations with love and caring.

This does not mean, however, a caregiver must be without limits, an-ger, or discipline. On the contrary, these are also important aspects, but they are carried out by example as well as disciplining the child in a calm, but firm and matter-of-fact manner without abuse or neglect. Love can now be associated with limits, values, nurturing, and appropriate expression of feelings. With these new associations, the child can learn to accept responsibility for his actions and make new choices. However, caregivers should be forewarned that the process takes a very long time.

Apology, Reparation, and Forgiveness

Apology, reparation, and forgiveness are also controversial concepts. Cloé Madanes (1995) has written extensively about her work in this area. She believes that apology and reparation are essential for the abuser/neglectful parent, but also for the healing of the child. The child can begin to understand that what happened to him was wrong and not his fault. When the abusive or neglectful parent is no longer available, substitute caregivers can express sadness for what the child has experienced. They can rewrite the story and promise to do what is needed to keep the child safe from this time forward.

While the work of Madanes (1995) does not require forgiveness, there is some emerging evidence that it may be physically and emotionally healthy to reach a state of forgiveness. While not a necessary component, I have found that in forgiving an abuser, understanding his/her humanity and frailty, a client is more able to forgive himself for whatever behaviors have caused him guilt. In all of this, each client needs to find some meaning for life. The child needs to have some good come from his suffering. This allows the integration of "lessons learned" into his future. This completes the grieving cycle and allows healing.

Developmental Attachment Work

Dr. Daniel A. Hughes (2003) talks about the need for children with

Disrupted Attachment Patterns to experience the cycle of conflict, resolution, and closeness. The therapist helps the family and the child to re-create this process with everyday experiences. With repetition and guidance, the child advances through the moral and emotional developmental stages. Use of the BOS (Braaten 1998) can also help assess and move youths through the developmental stages.

A Holistic Approach: Meet All of the Child's Needs

Since these children have multiple and complex needs, a therapist needs a systematized way of assessing a wide range of need areas. The CARE (Seifert 2003) was developed for just such a purpose. A wide array of areas is assessed, and a treatment or intervention plan is developed from the assessment for each area of need.

Motivational Interviewing

Taking responsibility for one's actions and making new choices is a part of motivational interviewing, based on the work of Carl Rogers. It involves going with the resistance, reframing goals, using one's own goals to reframe choices, commitment, and making a plan. It has been used primarily in addictions work, but can be very successful with this population, as well. The therapist says to the youth, *What do you want to be in your life?* The dialogue can go something like this:

> (Previously, the child has indicated his desire for a career.)
> **Child:** I can't stand my parents any more. I want to run away from home.
> **Therapist:** I hear you are unhappy with your parents. You really want to run away?
> **Youth:** Yes.
> **Therapist:** Oh, I get it, you want to be homeless, a street

bum, or a drug pusher. Is that it?

Youth: No, of course not, I want a career in ____.

Therapist: But how will running away get you to your goal?

Youth: I don't know.

Therapist: What can you do to help you achieve your goal of having a career in ____?

Youth: Trying to get along with my parents?

Therapist: Well, maybe it is worth a try. Let's figure out a plan to make this happen for you.

Trauma Work

Trauma therapy has been around for a long time and the techniques are well-known: desensitization, retelling the story, empowerment through changing the story, EMDR, psychodrama, and others. It is good to remember that attachment therapy is primarily trauma work. The difference is that the trauma may be pre-verbal and not remembered. Therefore, the story may need to be re-created from what is known.

Stages of Change

The Stages of Change by Prochaska, Norcross, and DiClemente (1994; APA Conference presentation by Dr. DiClemente 2006) is a conceptual framework for understanding the process of change. In the **Pre-contemplative Stage** — people are not interested in making a change. People insist that their behavior is acceptable. Many children with DAP are in this stage of change. Motivational interviewing may help here. In the **Contemplation Stage** they are thinking about changing their behavior. Those in this stage are apprehensive, in part because of past failures to change their behavior or ambivalence about change. In the **Preparation Stage**, they are ready to change their behavior within the next two weeks. Therapists should help with problem-solving, a plan, and support. In the **Action Stage**, they are actively changing their behavior. It is very important for therapists to follow up at critical points in the plan.

During the **Maintenance Stage**, clients maintain their changes. At this time, relapse prevention work is needed. When relapse occurs and is treated as a normal part of the process, the therapist can support the client in getting "back on track." Therapists help the client assess where he is in the stages of change and repeat previous steps. This process may take years for the youth with DAP.

Support and Education for Parents

Youth with Disrupted Attachment Patterns are difficult to parent. It is a tiring job that can make a caregiver, particularly the mom, feel that she is going crazy. Caregivers of these children need a considerable amount of education and support. They also need to be directly involved in the therapy of their child. Frequent respite is needed so that caregivers can have time for themselves. A support group is also helpful. Of course, funding for these activities is often problematic.

Accessing Pre-verbal Areas of Brain

Because much of abuse and neglect occurs pre-verbally, it is necessary to access pre-verbal areas of learning. This learning will necessarily be sensory, emotional, and kinesthetic. There may also be some state-dependent learning (i.e. things learned while crying or enraged that can only be changed when in that state). This is the conceptual framework behind rage-reduction therapies. Catharsis and emoting is probably important to the process, but there is little solid research to support it at this time. Non-verbal therapies such as art, movement, play therapy (explained in the book, *Theraplay: Helping Parents and Children Build Better Relationships through Attachment Based Play*, [Jernberg & Booth, 1999]), and dance may also be important for these youth, but again the jury is still out on this one, too.

Sensory Integration

Sensory integration is an area of specialty in the field of physical and occupational therapy. Because of severe neglect and abuse at critical stages of sensory development, there are often gaps and poor coordination among the different senses, causing problems with balance, noise tolerance, touch sensitivity, difficulty with self-soothing, and other sensory input problems. This is similar to what may be seen in Autism spectrum disorders. A physical or occupational therapist can be very helpful in this area.

Relationship Therapy

The problem with Disrupted Attachment Patterns is the effect they it has on relationships. All therapy is basically a form of relationship therapy. The therapist is using himself as part of a relationship to help change the internal working model of the client. You can only help (instruct, guide) change of the internal working model of a youth with Disrupted Attachment Patterns within the context of a nurturing relationship with good boundaries.

Animal Therapy

Some therapists have used healing techniques with animals such as dogs, horses, and dolphins for various therapies, including ones that treat Disrupted Attachment Patterns. Little research has been found on animal therapy within this population. It makes logical sense that the unconditional, positive love of animals might be helpful, but one must also watch for signs of animal cruelty.

Ideas for parents

Giving care for a child with DAP can be extremely challenging. Therapy for DAP kids is a combination of what the therapist does in the office and what the caregiver does at home. Both are essential pieces and neither can be ignored or neglected. The child can shred every bit of patience a parent may have, so here are a few suggestions for more successful results:

- **Every day is a new day** and a new opportunity for the child to experience success. It is through success that a child begins to develop a positive self-image. This supports the ability to follow rules and be reciprocal.

- It is extremely necessary for DAP caregivers to be **emotionally stable** themselves. If they have family of origin issues, therapy might be necessary for the caregivers.

- **Be even and calm** in your approach to discipline. Remember, you are trying to teach self-soothing and problem-solving. Use natural consequences, such as cleaning up their own messes, instead of punishment. Point out things like, *You can do a lousy job and work at it for an hour, or do a great job and be finished in 10 minutes.* Make consequences as immediate as possible. Avoid extremes in consequences that come from anger, as they are counter-productive.

- **Reinforcers should outnumber punishers by a ratio of four to one.** While many kids with DAP cannot yet benefit internally from rewards and punishment because of their lower level of moral development, the parent is picking up lost or skipped areas of development and trying to establish them.

A higher number of reinforcers helps parents keep a balance of positive-to-negative and not be overwhelmed with frustration. **Do not use physical punishment.**

- **Strict limits and boundaries** are needed. Children with DAP do better with lots of structure and routine. They often have difficulty with changes in routine and unstructured time. Give them plenty of warning before changing an activity or schedule.

- **Caregivers make the rules.** Children with DAP are afraid to allow adults to be in charge. Survival for them has been being in charge of their lives and not relying on adults to do anything for them. They want to make their own rules — clearly, you cannot allow them to do that. You must make the rules and stick to them. Initially, the caregiver needs to be in charge of everything: food, rules, and nurturing, and see that the child's needs are met. This is so the connection between parenting and meeting a child's needs can be made. Reciprocity begins and trust is built.

- **Give nurturing every day.** No matter how bad the day, spend some warm nurturing time with your child. This is the essential for bonding to take place. Without it, the therapy will not work. All children need generous amounts of love, affection, physical holding, positive activity, hugs, and kisses every day. Kids with DAP, although hard to love at times, need it more than most.

- **Insist on eye contact and truthfulness.** It is said that the eyes are the windows to the soul. Deep relationships are made through eye contact. Insist that the child look into your eyes when he talks to you. Have a non-verbal signal as a reminder. I put a single finger up in front of my nose and tap a couple of times. They know what that means: *Look into my eyes.*

- **Give them choices.** Help the child learn how to distinguish between good and bad choices. Help him learn how to make better choices. Do you want a fresh hot dinner now with the family or a cold one later by yourself? If he answers that he wants to eat with the family then say, *Great! I am glad you do. All you need to do is ____.* Make it contingent on washing his hands or setting the table, or whatever it is he is resisting. Remember, you are building compliance, so you want whatever he says to be compliant, no matter what he chooses. *Oh, you want to eat cold food by yourself with dirty hands. I thought so and was preparing for that, so go do some strong sitting while the family eats and when the food is good and cold, (exaggeration is good) I will call you. Don't forget to not wash your hands. There will be no one at the table to notice that you did not wash your hands. Thanks for being so compliant.* They don't get the answer they were looking for, which was anger and a fight. This seems to throw them off balance, see how silly they are being, and reconsider their choices.
- **Teach logic and problem-solving.** Remember, logic is often weak and needs to be taught. Talk them through problem-solving. This involves teaching sequences, deduction, and cause and effect.
- **Seek the help of a DAP-informed therapist**, someone who knows what you are up against.
- **Educate teachers** about DAP.
- **Take time for yourselves** as an individual and a couple.
- **Use respite** to give yourselves a break.

DAP is a very difficult and disturbing disorder with very negative consequences. It is very difficult to treat. It has the potential of pulling caregivers into being abusive and making themselves feel crazy. There is hope for curing a child of DAP if you find a therapist who is trained in the techniques that can help the child heal from trauma sufficiently to make new bonds.

Suggestions for Therapists

- A good therapist is a good therapist, regardless of theoretical orientation.
- If you are working with a child who has attachment problems, you should be informed about that area of work and seek to educate yourself.
- Guide and educate parents or caregivers.
- Use techniques that are within your comfort zone and area of expertise.
- Use supervision.

Hanging in for the Long Run

This process is not a short or easy one. These problems have been created on a very primitive level and will take a long time to alleviate, despite what managed care would have us believe. Many of these children have been in families that have had problems for generations. They won't be solved in a day or two — or even a month or two. Caregivers should not take these children in unless they plan to keep them for at least two years or more. Because these children are difficult to manage, they are often moved from one foster home or group placement to another, time after time. They do not have the chance to form attachment bonds in short-term placements. It probably takes at least two years in a stable environment for attachment bonds to form. That's a long time to fight the battle, day in and day out, but that's what it takes. It takes very special people and a lot of support and training to raise these children. It's not for everybody. There probably should be special foster care units for attachment dis-ordered children that include training, support, and periodic respite.

Therapists also should be able to work with the families for at least two years. One girl asked me if I would still be available to her when she was grown and had her own children. I told her that as long as I was still here (at my office), she could come see me. It gave her the long-term security she needed, whether she needs my services or not. I've seen another youngster off and on since she was 11. She is now a transition-age youth and I plan to see her periodically to help her adjust to being on her own.

Chapter 11

Treating Youth at High Risk for Violence

with a passage from Abigail S. Malcolm, Psy.D.

Dozens of different approaches to treatment for at-risk youth are being studied, and evaluations of their performance are now being reported (Blueprints). Some widespread and popular programs have fallen short, sadly. One prominent example is the Boot Camp programs — which are ineffective without accompanying cognitive-behavioral treatment, family involvement, and aftercare (Zaehringer 1998). Clearly, the most important question for those in charge with the care of possibly violent youth is simply, *What works?*

For many years, the common wisdom was that nothing worked in treating violent and chronically delinquent youths. However, recent research indicates a more encouraging view: not everything works *for every child*. Treatment is not a one-size-fits-all proposition. Goldstein and Glick (1987) discuss the idea of prescriptive programming that takes into account child and provider temperament, as well as program type. This individuation of treatment is only one element to expect from any successful treatment program.

There are several necessary program components of effective treatment. These would include continuous case management, family work, agency coordination, and emphasis on re-integration back into the community. Programs should address all problem areas. There must be clear and consistent consequences for misbehavior, and reinforcements should outnumber punishments by a ratio of four to one. The following are several treatments that I believe work well when administered by the appropriate professionals.

Community Mental Health and Treatment for Juveniles
Abigail S. Malcolm, Psy.D.

The discussion of youth and violence demands attention to the growing area of forensic mental health treatment for children and adolescents. Forensic mental health approaches, as Dr. Seifert has previously emphasized, will require critical attention across the lifespan of offenders. Unfortunately, attention in the form of empirically-validated research, academic literature, and evidence-based treatment on the subject matter is limited (Hartwell 2004). Many clinicians will recall the violence epidemic that plagued America's youth between the mid-1980's and the late 1990's (Snyder and Sickmund 1999). All too often the assumption made from declining prevalence rates leads to erroneous conclusions that youth are no longer exposed to and/or involved in violence.

One of the conclusions illuminated by the Department of

Health and Human Services, Substance Abuse and Mental Health Services Administration, Center for Mental Health Services (2002) includes facing the reality that the so-called "epidemic" of youth violence is not over and arrest rates are not accurately reflecting exposure and involvement. This same report highlights hope in treatment using both evidenced-based strategies and best practices, although the focus remains on prevention. There is no question that our society, our schools, and our communities need to embrace preventative approaches to youth violence. There is also no question that in the meantime, Community Mental Health Centers/Clinics (CMHC) are over-burdened with the responsibility for forensic treatment of juveniles.

Community Mental Health and Forensics: Making it Work

For those of you who have not had the humbling experience of community mental health, imagine the ambiance of an emergency room, but the cries you hear are for Depression and Schizophrenia rather than a broken arm or high fever. Then add an on-going struggle between limited necessities (such as money, space, qualified clinicians) and an abundance of needs (such Medicaid recipients, school-based mental health, state hospital referrals for indigent consumers). Although CMHC were created to serve the uninsured and under-served populations of our nation's mentally ill, literature suggests that less than 20 percent of those individuals and families are receiving services at CMCH; the primary explanation for this disparity is a lack of appropriate funding for the facing needs (Schiff et. al. 2003). Now, imagine your diligent community mental health clinician struggling to keep up her paperwork demands and continuing education credentials (not to mention her own checkbook), and on her desk is the referral for her next client: a 16- year-old male court-ordered for "treatment" with a history of depression.

Most clinicians working CMHC have been trained for the treatment of mental health disorders. They are confident in their ability and their dedication to community mental health is admirable. However, the majority of clinicians working in CMHC receive minimal education and training in forensic mental health, and most mental health clinics do not have systems in place that accommodate forensic clients. It is important to note the difference between Mental Health and Forensics, as they are all too often unfavorably merged. Mental health populations are comprised primarily of Axis I disorders, such as Bipolar Disorder, Schizophrenia, Major Depression, PTSD, and Anxiety Disorders. Daily functioning is on a continuum. Recovery is quick for some and slow for others and is also on a continuum. Well-controlled intermittent, mild to moderate episodes of a mood or anxiety disorder will not necessarily interfere with daily functioning. Someone with severe, chronic Schizophrenia requiring periodic hospitalizations and extensive community support will have impairment in daily functioning. Goals are often pro-social and involve being an active member of society.

A forensic population can be defined as having personality disorders, interpersonal difficulties, behavioral problems, and life-long courses of various levels of dysfunction or difficulty. Again, this population fills the full spectrum of effective daily functioning. However, social functioning is often impaired. There are issues of trust, appropriate relationships, ego1centrism, moral development, honesty, manipulation, and danger to others. They often have a negative view of themselves and others, especially authority figures. Moral development is often delayed leaving them at the egocentric stage of development. This means that what serves the self is what matters and empathy for others may not yet have developed. Their goals are often self-serving. The capacity to understand the importance of the best interest of the group through laws and rules that we voluntarily follow may not be well understood. Many, if not most, have histories of childhood abuse, neglect, or exposure to domestic violence.

The assessment and interventions with this population is necessarily different than those diagnosed with an interpersonal/developmental impairment. That is not to assume mental illness, including Axis II disorders, predicatively breed violence (U.S. Department of Health and Human Services 2002). The emphasis here is on the disparity between CMHC clinician trained in suicide risk assessment and assertiveness skill building, who are burdened with the treatment of forensic populations. The answers will hopefully ensue in future years of empirically-validated research and congresses of professionals who offer critical attention to the needs of both forensic mental health and CMHC. This type of attention will, no doubt, increase the professional value of these highly-trained therapists as integral professionals to our overall public health. Raising competence in clinicians begins with raising awareness. Providing assessment tools that cross the professions (i.e., from the CMHC clinician to the Department of Juvenile Services caseworker, to the school-based therapist, etc.) will raise the awareness to both the prevalence of youth violence and the risk.

Juvenile Risk Assessment and Community Mental Health Centers/Clinics

In a mental health population, assessment can effectively be done through instruments such as the MMPI-A, BASC, and MACI. These tools will clarify psychological dynamics and mental illness, if present. Self-report is not as much of an issue as it is in the forensic population, where third party verification is more important. However, when a youth has multiple problems, both mental health and forensic, a combination of tools is preferred. Forensic evaluation tools rely less on self-report because of the trust issues and because it is not always in the client's best interest to be completely truthful when court actions are pending. A person also has the right not to incriminate him or herself. Self-report assessment instruments can be used, but third party and official reports should also be used in the evaluation phase

*of a forensic assessment. Courts are concerned with pub-
lic safety, therefore, the need for tools that assess future
risk of dangerousness to others is also recommended. Risk
of future aggression and sexual behavior problems that
have been derived from statistical models should be part
of the evaluation since clinical assessment of risk of future
dangerousness is little (Quinsey, Harris, Rice, and Cormier
1998) better than chance. While risk assessments are not
perfect, they are better than clinical judgment in this area.*

*There are two specific concerns derived from the existent
knowledge of forensic assessment: (1) the ability of assessment to inform treatment; and (2) the accessibility of such
assessments to CMHC clinicians. The Association of Treatment of Sexual Abusers report, Managing Sex Offenders
in the Community: A National Overview (2003) repeatedly
focused on the integral role of assessment in effective
treatment of sexual offenders, including juvenile sexual
offenders. The Child and Adolescent Risk Evaluation (CARE,
described more effectively in previous chapters) readily
informs treatment with specific options (16 intervention
options) and case management steps of actions without
undermining validity or reliability (Nussbaum 2006). Since
the CARE does not require a doctorate level of psychology
to administer, it transcends professional levels of creden-
tialing and is available to all clinicians. Our CMHC centers
must be educated on the difference between psychological
evaluation, clinical judgment, and actuarial risk assess-*

ment. The goal of actuarial risk assessments, specifically in this context for juveniles, would be to raise clinical awareness and improve treatment.

It would seem, therefore, that CMHC clinicians indeed have accessibility to valid risk assessments that inform treatment. The appearance of quality clinical care is not always met with realistic steps for implementation. Financial concerns would be the first on any CMHC list of reasons why they cannot provide CARE packets to each of their clinicians for their use in assessment and treatment plan. There also remains the barrier that many clinicians face in gleaning background information from third parties about their forensic clients because their time is filled by high caseloads and an endless stream of paperwork. Although an essential step in forensic work, the public mental health system often does not have a mechanism to pay the clinic for collecting collateral information and consulting with teachers, extended family members, and employers. An assessment such as the CARE would require information about the degree of violence of past crimes committed and other background information. Picture our over-worked, underpaid CMHC clinician asking her new 16-year-old forensic client what degree assault he committed and if he had remorse for his crimes. Self-report of forensic clients is not enough; it is necessary to supplement a clinical interview (which ideally includes an actuarial risk assessment) with third party background information. The urgency of this matter not only influences treatment planning, but directly affects the personal safety of clinicians and CMHC staff.

Treatment Options for Juveniles in the Community

Treatment options of juveniles with mental illness in detention offers an accessible variety including group homes, hospitals, and other high-levels of clinical care. However, on the continuum of youth and violence, there are those offenders who have not been convicted, children who have the charges dropped due to their young age, juveniles who have been discharged from a group home, or the population dubbed "at-risk." The majority of these juveniles are referred to CMHC for treatment of their identified mental illness. Major mental illnesses, while often chronic, can often be very effectively treated with medication and therapy. At the higher functioning end of the continuum, therapy can be supportive, psychotherapeutic, family, or cognitive-behavioral. Therapists are trained to accept what the client presents; start where the client is functioning and how he or she sees the world. The clients are usually self-motivated and seek therapy voluntarily. They accept responsibility for their behaviors and for making changes in their lives. Use of a strengths model is often very effective. Many people recover fully and lead quite "normal," non-disrupted lives. When someone is on the lower end of the continuum, with major disruption in every day functioning (work and family), despite medication and therapy, major supports for housing, *jobs, and activities of daily living as well as medication are needed for a very long time, perhaps a lifetime. However, their life goals are often still pro-social.*

In the area of intervention, different approaches are needed for the forensic population. Some level of social and family dysfunction is generally intergenerational and lifelong. These clients are often court-ordered to an assessment or therapy, or they are having significant problems at work or within the family, causing others to seek assessment or therapy for them. They do not always accept responsibility for their actions or for changing. There are skill deficits that need to be addressed, such as social skills, anger management, and problem-solving. This population often has multiple problems so that Multi-systemic Therapy that approaches many areas that need to be addressed is often effective in treating the whole person (ATSA 2003). In addition to use of both group and individual therapy work focused on evidence-based practices and cognitive-behavioral techniques, juveniles may also require trauma therapies and/or family work. Just as risk assessment transcends the lifespan, so does the focus of treatment. Treatment planning for juveniles requires knowledge of developmental expectations, comprehension of forensic issues in treatment, proficiency in setting boundaries, extensive case management tasks... the list could continue for pages. When clients have issues in the mental health and forensic arenas, both approaches must be used to the possible extent.

Imagine now our CMHC clinician moments after she has completed her intake on the 16-year-old juvenile (which of course included the provision of third party background information from the Department of Juvenile Justice caseworker and the CARE): not only does she have to complete the necessary paperwork, contact the caseworker to collaborate care, and so on, but she also has to prepare a treatment plan that will assure authorization, coordinate with this juvenile's developmental capacity, and appropriately merge mental health care with forensic competency. Suggestions for intervention must be balanced with these capacities: (1) the capacity of mental health clinicians to forge into forensic work; (2) the capacity of CMHC to sustain clinicians who may feel their time would be better appreciated in private practice; (3) the capacity of CMHC to train and support clinicians in forensic mental health, developmental expectations, trauma work, etc.; and (4) the capacity for inter-disciplinary collaboration between CMHC and other agencies such as Juvenile Justice or local schools.

Clients in a mental health setting range from the single diagnosis of a major mental illness, to an interpersonal/developmental impairment, and/or forensic/legal issues, or all of the above. Recall again the CMHC clinician newly faced with a 16-year-old forensic client. Is it possible that the CMHC she works has a supply of CARE forms? Has she already been trained by her supervisor on the administration and scoring? Did she recently attend a state-funded training for clinicians focused on motivational interviewing in forensic treatment where she role-played how to balance strength-based treatment with pro-social expectations? When she gets to clinical team meeting that week (with a stack of paperwork and utilization management tasks to complete), was she advised that the clinic is now offering a group for juveniles with mental illness? The hope in critical questioning is to facilitate critical thinking.

While most youth who commit violence will not be arrested for violent crime (U.S. Department of Health and Human Services 2002), many of them will be directed to Community Mental Health Centers/Clinics either as part of their probation for a lesser charge, from school-based referral, or by other professionals. It is not enough to prepare our communities on how to prevent youth violence? We must prepare our CMHC on how to address the problems faced by continuing evidenced-based research on youth, violence, and treatment; offering clinicians actuarial assessment tools; supporting community mental health centers/clinics; and raising awareness toward mental health treatment of juveniles. When clinical and forensic competence merges with realistic and obtainable strategies, America's youth will have access to the care they deserve and clinicians will be appreciated for their thankless efforts.

Prenatal and Infancy Home Visitation by Nurses

Research by Office of Juvenile Justice and Delinquency Prevention (OJJDP) has demonstrated that visiting home nurses can increase bonding, improve care, and reduce future violence and child delinquency (Olds, Hill, and Rumsey 1998). The home visitors take child care and developmental information to parents. Healthy Families America is a nation-wide program of home visitors. Research on this program indicates positive outcomes, including reducing child abuse and neglect, improving healthy child development, greater school readiness, supporting family self-sufficiency, and increasing positive parenting.

The Blueprints for Violence Prevention, an initiative to identify violence prevention programs that are effective, modifies three major risk factors of future violence:

- Adverse maternal health-related behaviors during pregnancy
- Child abuse and neglect
- Adverse bonding experiences between mother and child

For more information visit *http://www.colorado.edu/cspv/blueprints/index.html* or contact *buhr-vogl.matthew@tchden.org*.

The following programs were taken from the Blueprints Initiative.

The Incredible Years Series
A part of the Blueprint program, The Incredible Years Series complete

curriculum, known as the Dina Dinosaur Program, targets youths ages two through eight. It promotes social competence and prevents, reduces, and treats conduct problems in children.

For more information, visit *www.incredibleyears.com* or contact *incredibleyears@seanet.com.*

Promoting Alternative Thinking Strategies (PATHS)

PATHS is a school-based program that is taught by teachers in kindergarten through grade five as part of the regular curriculum. It focuses on self-control, emotional understanding, self-esteem, relationships, and interpersonal problem-solving skills. For more information, visit *www.prevention.psu.edu* or contact *prevention@psu.edu.*

Bullying Prevention Program

Bullying is a significant problem in schools worldwide. The Bullying Prevention Program's goal is to reduce bullying among school students. There are three phases of the program:

1. An anonymous questionnaire evaluates the extent of the problem. A school committee forms a plan of action and children are supervised during breaks.
2. Rules that prohibit bullying are introduced and enforced. Classroom meetings are held and parents are encouraged to participate.

3. Interventions with bullies, victims, and their parents are held.

For more information contact *olweus@psych.uib.no.*

Big Brothers and Sisters of America

Big Brothers and Big Sisters is one of the best-known mentoring programs in the U.S. It provides over 100,000 one-on-one relationships for at-risk youth. In an 18-month study, youth in BBBS were 46 percent less likely to start using drugs, 27 percent less likely to start drinking, and 32 percent less likely to hit someone. School performance and peer and family relationships were also improved. For more information, go to *http://www.bbbsa.org.*

Life Skills Training (LST)

It is well-known that many children with behavior problems lack general life and social skills. LST targets psychosocial factors and skills known to be associated with behavior problems and drug and alcohol abuse. The programs provide drug resistance skills and life skills to middle school students. It has been found to cut alcohol, tobacco, and marijuana use by 50 to 75 percent. Follow-up studies indicate reductions can last through the twelfth grade. For more information, go to *http://www.lifeskillstraining.com.*

Functional Family Therapy (FFT)

FFT is a short-term, well-documented program that uses multi-systemic techniques. This program is basically a family therapy approach that includes most, if not all, family members. By examining the systems (i.e. schools, churches, jobs) in which each family member participates, the therapist and the team make a plan that will build on family strengths and problem-solve any difficulties. Long-term research — this program has been studied for 25 years — has shown reductions in youth re-offending and sibling entry into offending during one-, three-, and five-year follow-up studies. Cost comparisons show that the program is cost-effective. In one evaluation site, 80 percent of families completed treatment. Youth in 20 percent of those families re-offended, compared to 36 percent in the comparison group. FFT costs $1,000 per family or less for a two-year period, while a residential placement will often cost over $13,000. More information can be found at *http://www.fftinc.com*.

Multisystemic Therapy (MST)

MST targets the multiple factors that can contribute to antisocial behavior, and uses the strengths of each youth's social networks to promote positive change for the youth. Interventions include strategic and structural family therapy, behavioral parent training, and cognitive-behavioral therapies. MST also addresses barriers to effective parenting. Therapists are available 24 hours a day, seven days a week. School/vocational interventions target skills for future employment. Duration of treatment is four months and involves approximately 60 hours of service. Research has demonstrated 25 to 75 percent reductions in re-arrest and 47 to 64 percent reductions in out-of-home placements for as much as four years. The program has also proven to be cost-effective. The website for MST is *http://www.mstservices.com*.

Dialectical Behavioral Therapy (DBT)

Dr. Marsha Linehan developed DBT as a therapy to work with clients with Borderline Personality Disorder. It is evidence-based and involves increasing skills in the areas of interpersonal, self-soothing, affect regulation, and self-monitoring behaviors. Validation strategies are interwoven with traditional cognitive-behavioral techniques for change. Targets for therapy are behaviors that are life-threatening, interfere with therapy, decrease the quality of life, and promote ineffective coping. Although I haven't used this technique enough myself to vouch for its effectiveness, I am convinced that it holds hope for this population because it deals with the core issues. Dr. Alec Miller had a book come out in November 2006 from Guilford that applies Dr. Linehan's DBT principles to adolescents with behavioral problems. For more information go to this website: *http://www.behavioraltech.org*.

Multi-modal Treatment

Multi-modal treatment that meets the community, family, social, cognitive, emotional, personal, and educational needs of the child is important. The various risk factors need to be assessed and addressed. Some studies found that behavioral treatments show larger effect sizes than humanistic and family-based treatments, which have better results than individual psychodynamic interventions (Roth and Fonagy 1996). Treatment should target the child's needs. For example, cognitive/behavioral treatment and skill-oriented programs can address problem-solving, empathy building, anger management, self-soothing, and reality testing. Contingency management programs can reinforce pro-social skills and competencies. Meanwhile, it is also important to target criminogenic factors, such as deviant peers, lack of empathy, the importance of rules, and the social order. However, it should be understood that this is a lower level of moral development, and earlier stages of development must be addressed before moving on to skills for higher levels of moral development. The Behavioral Objective Sequence (Braaten 1998) is a very effective tool for assessing developmental skill levels.

The frequency of mental health and substance abuse disorders among violent youth is higher than that of the general community, and these risk factors should be assessed early. The juvenile justice system and the mental health system need to work together to find and treat children with both mental health problems and behavioral acting-0 out. Aggressive children often have school and learning problems that need to be addressed at the source. At home, we need to help families change and become healthy and effective. We must treat the *whole* child and family.

While there are many evaluations of programs to reduce delinquency, programs addressing violence are very limited. Tolan and Guerra (1994), in their analysis of the youth violence intervention literature, indicate that multidimensional cognitive-behavioral programs are effective in community interventions, especially when targeting younger children and their families. These programs should include externally imposed structure, stimulation control, individual goals for improvement, behavioral contracting, and consistent, repeated contingency reinforcement for pro-social behavior.

Multidimensional Treatment Foster Care (MTFC)

MTFC recruits, trains, and supervises foster parents to provide children with appropriate supervision, discipline, limits, and a positive relationship with an adult. Youth progress through a level system based on their behavior. If the youth is to return home, the same training is given to the caregivers in the child's home. Case Managers maintain close contact with MTFC parents. MTFC has demonstrated reduced out-of-home placement and fewer arrests for those participating in the program when compared to the control group. The website, *http://www.oslc.org*, can provide additional information.

Quantum Opportunities Program (QOP)

The QOP provides an array of services and relationships among peers while they are in high school. The program provides youth with pro-social activities, skill enhancement, and reinforcement for positive actions. A coordinator works with a small (no more than 25) group of youths. Participants were more likely to finish high school and enroll in higher education, and were less likely to be a teen parent or be arrested. Their web site is *http://www.oicworld.org*.

Parent Management Training (PMT)

PMT is a therapy whereby the therapist works with the parents to develop effective interventions. It has been found to be effective during and after treatment to reduce delinquent and disruptive behaviors for as many as 14 years following treatment. Problem-solving Skills Training (PSST) has been found to be effective, especially when in combination with PMT (Roth and Fonagy 1996).

Preschools Programs with Parent Involvement

Good early childhood prevention programs are Head Start or the Perry Point Project, which involve family members in programs that prevent addicted mothers from using drugs and alcohol while pregnant and help them bond with their children.

Residential Programs

Institutional programs that include building interpersonal skills, family effectiveness training, family involvement and therapy, cognitive/behavioral treatment, and multiple other services are able to increase children's pro-social behaviors. Zigler, Taussig, and Black (1992) and Tolan and Guerra (1994) found that long-term family interventions (one year or more) were effective for troubled youths.

Other Programs

Other programs include targeting high-risk youth, beginning services early, stopping child abuse and neglect, making mental health and substance abuse treatment readily available to children and parents, school anti-drug and alcohol programs, promoting responsible, non-violent behavior, and increasing the number of conflict resolution and anger management skills programs. Research has demonstrated that popular programs such as *The Second Step: A Violence Prevention Curriculum* can produce a moderate decrease in aggressive behavior and an increase in pro-social behavior (Grossman et al. 1997). Mentoring has also been found to be an effective strategy (Grossman and Garry 1997). School-based programs are becoming more widely accepted. These programs place services in schools where children spend most of their days and have frequent problems. It is important to coordinate these services with teachers and parents.

Our discussion would not be complete without considering some of the newer programs that show some promise but need additional research to establish their value. Abused children, especially those who have been sexually abused, often have a set of characteristics that cause them to be less effective in dealing with the problems of everyday living. They sometimes have attachment disorders or problems. We also know that many addicted women who are unable to stay clean and sober have unresolved sexual abuse issues, and many violent offenders were abused as children. Therefore, therapy, which addresses the abuse issues, needs to be developed and tested. There is good preliminary success with a program developed at the Family Therapy Institute of Washington, DC. Eye Movement Desensitization

Reprocessing (EMDR), developed by Shapiro, is a promising trauma therapy. Psychodrama is a trauma resolution technique developed in part by Mareno. All of these programs, again, need more study.

Presently, there is not an organized effort to identify the children with risk factors for future violence at a young age and provide multimodal interventions for these children in the community and family. This would require a partnership among daycare centers, schools, mental health, addiction treatment, and public healthcare providers, departments of juvenile justice, child protective agencies, churches, and community organizations. Agencies should provide multiple services to families with risk factors such as violence, alcoholism, criminality, and drug abuse. A tool, such as the CARV or SAVRY, for early identification of kids at greater risk is also needed. Research to develop effective early interventions is also important.

Prevention will involve stopping domestic violence and child abuse. We must hold the perpetrators of family aggression accountable, court-order treatment, and enforce protection orders. The partners, as well as the children of violent families, need treatment to recover from domestic violence. We also need programs to help the children in families where there is chronic substance abuse, severe untreated mental illness, or criminal behavior.

Chapter 12

A Promising Practice for the Future: School-Based Mental Health

By Rob Schmidt, LCPC, NCC

As we have seen in previous chapters, violence is related to trauma and mental health, family, and substance abuse issues. Treatment for all of these issues can be provided through the public and private mental health system. For communities to break the cycle of violence, social disengagement, and psychological deterioration, effective prevention and intervention programs must be made readily available to our children and youth. When we begin thinking about where to institutionalize prevention and intervention programs, one common denominator for our youth would be our schools. Schools provide the unconditional support, structure, and safe environment for effective implementation and program monitoring. The public school system is in the community (neighborhood) and is an ideal place in which to provide increased and expanded student supportive services that would benefit the child, family, and school system. One such program that combines both prevention and intervention services is School-Based Mental Health (SBMH).

What is known is that our youth need increased support and mental health services now more than ever. The psychological, family, and neighborhood problems and stress affecting our young people today has become increasingly overwhelming for not only our school systems but also for our Juvenile Justice Systems. Teachers are well aware that when children and teens are focused on problems at home or within themselves, they often do not do well in school.

Educational institutions are finding that they must provide increased student supportive services and programs that address such complex needs, because they affect school performance goals and objectives. The perfect teacher, administrative staff, and best-laid curriculum plans simply are not enough for a youth with issues relating to mental health, trauma, substance abuse, violence, Disrupted Attachment Patterns, or family problems. School systems across the nation are providing the means for children to learn, and although capable, they are not succeeding. School success and good mental health are *intrinsically* tied together and essential for violence reduction.

A general reminder of the prevalence and history of our children's mental health issues and needs are included below. These numbers will, I hope, allow for a greater understanding of how we perpetually continue to not meet these needs, as well as why schools pose as our only unified venue to provide preventative and intervention services.

Acknowledging the Need

It was 1966, and one of the earlier pioneers on researching the profound impact of school-based mental services on students and schools of the 1950s, Dr. Patricia Crowther, took the stage and began

addressing the teachers and staff of the Philadelphia Public School's
District 3:

> Recent surveys have shown that at least 13 percent of the
> American school population shows evidence of ... deviant pat-
> terns of growth and development and maladaptive behavior
> in varying degrees of severity. One of the most pressing and
> plaguing problems presented to educators is the ever-increas-
> ing number of children, who despite an inherent ability to
> learn are not benefiting from a regular classroom teaching
> experience as shown by their continuing academic under-
> achievement.

> We are all aware of the excitement and enthusiasm of the
> kindergarten child, slowly turning to apathy and despair as he
> progresses through the elementary years. We are also aware
> of the dropouts and failures in the secondary years. What
> ever happens?

Fifteen years later, it was estimated that 15 percent of all school-
age children displayed deviant behavior characteristics of mental
disorders, which seriously interfere with social and emotional development and learning (Bloom 1981). Some 20 years after that, the
former Surgeon General, David Satcher, included in his 1999 Mental
Health Report on Children and Mental Health, "The burden of suffering experienced by children with mental health needs and their
families has created a health crisis in this country." What we know in
2006, spanning 40 years of enlightened awareness, is that our children's mental health continues to be a serious problem. The mental
health needs of our children remains in a crisis state, compounded by

the multiple barriers and complexities encountered by children and families seeking access to quality care, insurance, transportation, and following through on community services.

National statistics included in Satcher's report introduced the following figures on the deterioration of today's children: approximately one in five children and adolescents (20 percent) experience the signs and symptoms of a DSM IV (Diagnostic and Statistical Manual) disorder during the course of a year; one in ten children suffers from mental illness. Twenty-one percent of all children and adolescents ages 9 to 17 suffer from a diagnosable mental or addictive disorder, and 12 to 22 percent of all children suffer from mental, emotional, or behavioral disorders. Half of this number is estimated to have problems with violence. One-third of one percent of juveniles ages 10 to 17 are arrested for a violent crime.

According to the National Center for Mental Health and Juvenile Justice, these children are estimated to have mild to severe emotional or behavioral problems that interfere with their daily functioning (Cocozza and Skowyra 2000). When we think in terms of where a child spends most of his daily functioning during the course of a year, it's in school. Therefore, it's clear that behavioral health problems affect many children and adolescents' ability to function in school. So not only do we have a child suffering from deep emotional pain, but now we also have a child outwardly showing signs of distress, being suspended from school, receiving decreased grades, disciplinary referrals, and attending school only sporadically.

What is most disturbing is that, according to the Children's Defense

Fund, less than one third of children under age 18 with a serious disturbance receive any mental health services. Often, the services they do receive are inappropriate (Children's Defense Fund, CMHS — Mental Health, US 1994). Generally, only 16 percent of all children receive any mental health services and of that same 16 percent, 70 to 80 percent receive that care in a school setting, as noted by the Center for Health Care and Health Care in Schools (Rones M and Hoagwood K. 2000; BJ Burns, Costello EJ, Angold A, Tweed D et al. 1995). According to Dr. Mark Weist of the University of Maryland's National Center for School Mental Health Analysis in Action, fewer than 10 percent of all school districts in the United States currently have an established School Based Mental Health Program (M. Weist 1999).

In the United States alone, we are losing 4,000 youth to suicide every year (Suicide Prevention Action Network, SPAN, 2005). In a typical high school classroom, it's likely that at least three students have made a suicide attempt within the past year (Center For Disease Control). To coincide with this, the CDC has also reported that 16.9 percent of students in grades 9 to 12 have seriously considered attempting suicide within the past 12 months. In a U.S. Government Survey in 2000, it was estimated that 3 million children ages 12 to 17 considered suicide, with more than a third actually attempting suicide.

The presented national statistics are discouraging. What is happening to America's children? Dr. Patricia Crowther posed this same question in 1966. Maybe our children are simply sending us a signal that the amount of adult stressors, expectations, and pressures placed on them is just too much too soon. Common stressors may include:

- The breakdown of (or lack of) family and support
- Exposure to violence on the streets, through video games and television, and, most unfortunately, in the home
- Peer pressure
- Drugs
- School Pressure

Our fast-paced society is leaving the emotional needs of our children behind, and without this very basic primal development, schools and societal norms are trying to build on a fractured foundation.

There are many pitfalls that await children whose mental health needs remain unmet, such as increased dropout rates, increase risk of drug addiction and experimentation, broken relationships, and crime. In 1991, juveniles between the ages 12 and 19 (grades 7 to 12) were responsible for 19 percent of all violent crime in the U.S. It is important to note that only half of all juvenile crime is reported to law enforcement, and crime by children under age 12 is not included in these statistics at all, due to a variety of factors, including problems with reporting information on minors (OJJDP September 1999). This last group, unfortunately, is the largest/fastest growing segment of the juvenile offending population.

Again, serious, violent juvenile offenders begin having behavior problems around age 7 (third grade), while the average age of their first contact with juvenile justice authorities is 14 (eighth to ninth grade). Youth in the juvenile justice system experience substantially higher rates of mental health disorders than youth in the general population. This is a major conclusion drawn from a review of 34 studies (Otto 1992; Cocozza 2000).

These are the same school-aged children who, in all likelihood, displayed maladaptive behaviors and presented psychological symptoms within the classroom. Usually, decreased school performance is the first warning signal that something in the child's life is breaking down. These indicators include (as noted earlier): decreased attendance, grades, increased suspensions, and disciplinary referrals. These are the earliest warning signs to school staff that a child is emotionally troubled. If these needs remain unmet, the school, child, and family fail.

We must also be aware of a factor often overlooked, that by the time a child enters school, he/she has already lived an extensive developmental life, which may predispose the child to future mental health needs. Services provided within the school setting may be the only opportunity for a child to be identified for and receive early prevention/intervention program services. Early/first interveners such as teachers, custodians, secretaries, principals, guidance counselors, and school nurses may be the only hope in identifying students to receive mental health services.

One of the most frustrating experiences for any classroom teacher is having a student of average or better-than-average intellectual ability, who does not successfully achieve his/her academic potential. It's hard to teach a child academically when his basic needs are not being met either physically or emotionally. So many extraneous variables come into play that present as the biggest roadblocks to student learning and success.

Chart 10: The most common mental health issues for child and adolescents today according to Olbrich, S., Children's Mental Health (2002) are:

Disorder	Number of Children Affected
Anxiety	8-10 per 100
Conduct	7 per 100
Depression	6 per 100
Learning	5 per 100
Attention	5 per 100
Eating	1 per 150
Substance Abuse	Unknown

The question is, do we spend a little time and money now, in the primary years of a child's life, for prevention and intervention, or spend a lot more during the teen's secondary years in the juvenile justice system? And even more in state facilities, and yet again in the cost of compiling even more victims, who may perpetuate the cycle of violence? The unfortunate reality check is that under national, state, or local budget constraints, prevention programs are the first to lose funding. So instead of spending thousands on prevention/intervention programs annually to institutionalize promising practices, millions if not billions are spent annually in rehabilitative programs, uninsured visits to the emergency room, failing educational systems, jails, prisons, and the like.

Promising Practice

I remember being in attendance at one school's "Opening Day" ceremony, which addressed all school district personnel, including bus drivers, teachers, cafeteria workers, security staff, and administrators. The guest speaker, Dr. Larry Bell, left an everlasting message, one I think of daily, "...That even on your worst day, you may be a child's only best hope."

For some children and youth, schools may be the only stable, unconditional environment they have in their early lives. Without a stable social/emotional atmosphere, individual academic success will continue to be a struggle for students, families, and schools. There are some school districts in the United States that are realizing the true benefits for the improved social/emotional well-being of the student and family as evident by improved school performance after program implementation.

Families choose school-based services over outpatient settings more often, due to the fact that services available at school drastically decrease the barriers that block traditional mental health treatment — the chief barrier being transportation. This is the most cost-effective means of treatment and, for some families, school is the only place their child may receive physical/mental health care.

A rural school district in Maryland is fortunate to offer comprehensive school-based mental health services that are voluntarily available to all students and families. Most importantly, this specific program is outcomes/researched-based and has received national attention.

These services originally began as apart of the Safe Schools/Healthy Students Grant that began in 1999 and ended September of 2003. It has developed into a self-sustainable national model program with over seven years of outcomes data (Seifert 2006).

This program centers around two basic objectives: 1) Decrease the child's initial presenting symptoms; 2) Increase school performance. It is designed to provide the earliest forms of prevention and intervention services for students and their families in grades prekindergarten to 12th grade.

Services include pre/post testing using the Behavior Assessment Scale for Children, Individual (BASC), family and group therapy, intensive outpatient program, psychiatric rehabilitative program, psychiatrist-led evaluations/consults, and crisis assessments. Pre/post academic monitoring is also a part of the comprehensive program. In-service trainings are also offered to teachers and staff on school-selected topics related to better understanding children's mental health needs, signs and symptoms, and how to make referrals for increased student supportive assistance.

These school-based mental health services provide immediate access for students and families, and allow for the coordination between the child's therapist, teacher, and parent to work in unison toward academic goals and social emotional development. It allows for the most important people in the child's life to be on the same team. Most importantly, because school-based mental health services are so readily accessible, it is literally breaking down the wall of stigma that too often keeps families from accepting services.

Outcomes

Referrals to the program come typically from the first intervener in a child's life, such as teachers, guidance counselors, student support teams, community agencies, wellness centers, parents, principals, and the students themselves. All referrals are forwarded to the mental health "gate-keeper" who then contacts the legal guardians and shares available services at school and in the community.

With seven consecutive years of study from 1999 to 2006, based on 1,655 school-based mental health referrals, the following summary of our findings are listed below:

- 80 percent of the families chose school-based mental health services over private providers or community agencies.
- 38 percent of the 1,655 SBMH Referrals originated by the guidance counselor.
- October and February were the most referred months.
- Grades six and nine were the most referred grades.
- Ninth grade white females were the most referred race, gender, and grade.
- Reasons for referral: 36 percent depressive symptoms; 27 percent family problems; 22 percent behavior problems; 7 percent grief loss; and 8 percent other.

Comparing (n = 632) Program Participants (PP) vs Non Participants (NP):

Disciplinary Referrals

Year 1

>   PP decreased disciplinary referrals by 45 percent
>
>   NP increased disciplinary referrals by 46 percent

Year 2

>   PP decreased disciplinary referrals by 40 percent
>
>   NP increased disciplinary referrals by 48 percent

As a comparison, overall arrests for violent crimes for youth ages 10-17 in Talbot County from 1995 to 2003 declined from 135 per 10,000 youth to 82 per 10,000 youth and non-violent juvenile arrest rates went from 346 to 282 (2006 Kids Count Maryland).

Attendance

Year 1

>   PP increased attendance rate by 56 percent
>
>   NP recorded decreased attendance by 66 percent

Year 2

>   PP increased attendance by 57 percent
>
>   NP decreased attendance by 59 percent

Suspensions

Year 1

>   PP decreased suspensions by 32 percent
>
>   NP increased suspensions by 33 percent

Year 2

>   PP decreased suspensions by 27 percent
>
>   NP increased suspensions by 16 percent

Pre/Post Testing — Using the BASC

Student Self-Reports (n = 362) comparing Before (B)/After (A) treatment resulted in clinical significance in all four categories:

> School Maladjustment — B — 52.76 / A — 50.87
>
> Clinical Maladjustment — B — 53.03 / A — 48.32
>
> Personal Adjustment — B — 45.44 / A — 48.89
>
> Emotional Symptom Index — B — 54.04 / A — 48.69

It's important to note that included in the sub-clusters, clinically significant reductions were recorded in: Anxiety, Depression, and Somatic; increases in student Self-Esteem and Self-Reliance were also recorded.

The outcomes provided by this comprehensive program is ongoing and year-round, and presents as a promising practice with hopes of being duplicated to prove the efficacy and impact that such programs can have on our children, family, and schools. School programs must be recognized and available to all students, instead of the traditional method of only offering mental health services at school to students that qualify for Special Education.

What we found in the outcomes for this program is that all students are susceptible and vulnerable to life events that would warrant intervention services. We sometimes use the "at-risk" phrase to identify groups who would more typically access services. Students from the very wealthy to the very poor are presented with very similar problems or unforeseen life circumstances. The only difference through school-based mental health is that both had equal access to receive services.

Again, everyone benefits from these prevention and intervention programs. We need more school-based mental health programs that are outcome and research-based. If schools are to meet their own local, state, and national mandated educational goals, they must provide expanded supportive services to include school-based mental health services. School success, reduced behavior problems, and good mental health are *intrinsically* tied together.

M y colleagues in the fields of mental health, psychology, and criminal justice and I have come a long way since the years when we had to rely on clinical judgment and the degree to which our hair stood on end to know whether a patient would again resort to violence. I know I have burnt plenty of midnight oil in my own quest to develop actuarial risk tools and youth and adult violence assessments, such as the CARE, that will give caretakers and authorities the information they need to intervene in the correct manner. However, we are still merely peeking through the fronds of a wilderness that will demand a greater deal of exploration.

Along with further clinical research, it will take a collective worldwide effort to stop the generational cycle of violence that germinates as far away as the desert caves of Afghanistan, the rowdy streets of Rio de Janeiro, the crowded brothels in India, and the unsuspecting middle schools in Hometown, USA. In all these places, children have been left behind. Attachments between child and caregiver were disrupted, destroyed, or never allowed to form in the first place. Their attachments may have been disturbed because of abuse, severe neglect, or exposure to domestic or community violence, which we know inevitably leads to emotional, physical, cognitive, moral, social, and spiritual problems when untreated. Even when there are parents around, lives spent in constant states of war and oppression are disaster-prone from the get-go. The results are burgeoning terrorist organizations, cults, and gangs, which are attracting these young souls, desperate for acceptance and companionship, in startling numbers.

When Disrupted Attachment Patterns are severe. They result in conduct and personality disorders and violence. A child with DAP will not have empathy for others, a need to follow the rules of authority or society, or even a conscience — thus we have people like Ted Kaczynski, Charles Manson, David Berkowitz, and Ted Bundy. While these children can be identified and treated as early as 2 years old, the problem is generally not addressed — if addressed at all — until later adolescence and adulthood.

There are many treatments that attempt to address DAP. All are complex, long-term, and must involve the caregiver. The caregiver must have a certain level of maturity so that they are not drawn into an abusive cycle themselves. Because there are so many treatments, the one employed must be adequate and may need to be provided in conjunction with another treatment. Disrupted attachment, personality disorders, and psychopathy are related in some way, and though we do not yet know exactly how, future research should illuminate the answer. It's ironic to think that we build more and invest more in prisons to house those who harm others than we do to provide violence treatment and prevention programs. In the next few years, however, if we can invest in therapy so that it is more developed and readily available, we will reduce crime and violence that prisons have only been able to contain for the short-term.

While society and the fields that study violence have a long way to go, much progress is being made. Research is helping to define and elucidate the theory of the development of violent behaviors. Studies of the various risk tools will also improve our ability to predict future risk. Development of clinical tools will assist in creating intervention plans. An important development is the use of a case management tool that helps determine the intensity and type of services needed. This can be used to determine youth at risk at an earlier age so that there is a greater opportunity for interventions to be effective before severe and chronic violent behaviors are entrenched patterns that lead to incarceration.

Many other youth assessment tools are in the developmental or research stages. It is likely that several tools will be used simultaneously because each uses a slightly different risk perspective and may provide unique information. Comparing tools allows a practitioner to choose the tool that best suits his or her population and situation. Most of the traditional risk tools do not include case or risk management tools. Older tools have more peer review and cross-validation studies than newer tools. However, some of the newer tools are showing stronger constructive and predictive validity than some of the older tools.

Studies of the various risk assessment tools have found differences in their ability to predict future violence. Research on risk evaluation tools has determined that we can improve the prediction of future violence significantly over unaided clinical judgment by using tools developed from statistical analysis of the traits of violent offenders. In general, there have been four stages thus far in the development of risk evaluation tools. The fourth generation of tools uses clinical items, dynamic and resiliency factors, and risk management plans. Of the youth risk tools reviewed, the CARE included suggested interventions that can manage and reduce the risk of future severe behavior problems.

Harknett et al. (2005) examined the relationship between public expenditures on children and child outcomes. They found that public expenditures on children are related to better child outcomes across a wide range of indicators, including measures of child mortality, elementary school test scores, and adolescent behavioral outcomes. States that spend more on children, in programs such as School-Based Mental Health, have better child outcomes even after taking into account a number of potential confounding influences. The sensitivity analyses suggest that the results presented may be conservative, yet the findings reveal a strong relationship between state generosity toward children and children's well-being. This means that good prevention of youth and adult behavioral problems will be directly proportional to the amount of money invested in children's services.

We must continue to recognize, diagnose, and provide appropriate treatment to those displaying Disrupted Attachment Patterns warning signs. Therapists of children or teens with attachment problems, through various modalities, must help youth to understand and cope more effectively with life by employing nurturing, explanations, and setting firm boundaries that accept the child but not the behavior. The work may include teaching caregivers nurturing touch techniques, psychodrama, sensory integration, bilateral physical and sensory experience, healing from loss, finding meaning in life, trauma work, and retelling their stories to form the basis of emotional, spiritual, and existential healing. All of this prevention and treatment is worth every penny if it can spare one child from hurting others, growing into a dangerous adult, and spending the rest of his life between those miserable Walls.

Acknowledgements

I want to acknowledge and thank my husband, Rick, for reading the book 10 times as well as Deana Krizan, Dr. Phil Rich, Gerry Blasingame, and Dr. Kenneth Maton for reading the draft book and providing comments. Rob Schmidt and Dr. Abigail Morgan both contributed sections which enhanced the book greatly, and I thank them. My son, John Wright, and my friend's mother, Peg Phillips, proofread the pre-publication version and gave me great feedback. Each contribution made the book better than it would have been without it. But, for more than what all of these people did, I want to thank them for being friends, supporters, and colleagues. What a great crew I have!

I have many to thank, for there are many who have helped me arrive at this point in my life. I am also grateful to the rest of my family for their understanding my need to work hard for many years in a field that is often dangerous. I love you all very much. Two of my sisters, Cindy Love and Linda Williams, helped me gather and write family memories for this book. To them and to my other sisters, Nancy Foxwell and Marcia Palmer, the twins, I say, *Thanks for the wonderful memories!* To my parents, grandparents, aunts, uncles, and family friends who helped raise me, I can't begin to thank you enough.

My friends, Sarah Hooper and Lynn Gavigan, have given me support, ideas, encouragement, and mountains of help over the years. They run ESPS and work tirelessly, and I can never thank them enough. Mary Britton has been a tireless assistant for many years and deserves many thanks. I thank my mother and my grandmother; I have tried to follow in their footsteps as a strong, intelligent, ethical woman.

I thank my editors, Carolyn McKibbin and Elizabeth Nollner from Acanthus Publishing, for their hard work and for making this book much better than it ever could have been without them. I thank Paige Stover Hague at The Ictus Initiative for her wonderful guidance and her fantastic team, George Kasparian, Julie Reilly, Domonic Gunn, Sarah Martin, MaDonna Johantgen, and Tony Manes; without them this book would not exist. A special thanks to Dr. David Nussbaum, who has been a colleague and a supporter of my work for many years, helped edit this book, and wrote the forward.

I owe my life and my safety to the correctional staff at the various facilities at which I've worked. They intervened in confrontations that put my life at risk, and they taught me the hard facts about prison life one cannot learn in school books. I thank my clients who have also taught me much. Without their time, patience, and dedication, many lessons I learned would never have taken place. I thank Gina Harvey for showing me the Philippines and Zosie Semense for taking care of my Filipino babies.

I pray that people worldwide will step in to protect and heal the children who have been abused, neglected, or exposed to domestic violence so that their course can detour to a path that is good and prosperous. If this book stops one violent act, it has been worth the effort — but I hope it does much more. Thank you for reading.

PRAYER FOR PEACE

I pray to God above
For patience and for love.
He guides my steps below
And watches as I go.
I say a prayer for peace.
For all in the Middle East.
With light from above,
Let us join our hearts with love.
Pray for peace throughout the world,
Let Love's banner be unfurled
In Lebanon and Africa,
Israel, Europe, and America.

References

Achenbach, T.M. 1991. *Manual for the Child Behavior Checklist/4-18 and 1991 Profile*. Burlington, VT: University of Vermont, Department of Psychiatry.

Allen, Hauser, and Borman-Spurrell. 1996. Attachment theory as a framework for understanding sequelae of severe adolescent psychopathology: an 11-year follow-up study. University of Virginia.

American Academy of Child and Adolescent Psychiatry. 1999. Practice parameters for the assessment and treatment of children and adolescents who are sexually abusive of others. *Journal of the American Academy of Child and Adolescent Psychiatry* 38: 12 (Suppl. December), 55s-76s.

———. 2004. Child and Adolescent Service Intensity Instrument, *CASII User's Manual*. Washington, D.C., American Academy of Child and Adolescent Psychiatry, 3615 Wisconsin Ave., Washington, D.C. 20016-3007, www.aacap.org.

American Association of Community Psychiatrists. 1999. http://www.wpic.pitt.edu/AACP/finds/CALOCUSv15.pdf.

American Psychological Association. 1999. Standards for Educational and Psychological Testing.

Andrews, D.A. and J.L. Bonta. 1995, 1998. *LSI-R: Level of Service Inventory-Revised, User's Manual.* Toronto: Multi-Health Systems, Inc.

Association for Treatment of Sexual Abusers. 2003. *Managing Sex Offenders in the Community: A National Overview.* Eugene, Oregon: http://www/atsa.com/researchcomp.html.

Augimeri, L.K., C.D. Webster, C.J. Koegl, and K.S. Levene. 1998. *Early Assessment of Risk for Boys, EARL-20B, Version 1, Consultation Edition.* Toronto: Earlscourt Child and Family Centre.

Barbaree, H. E., M. C. Seto, C. M. Langton, and E. J. Peacock. 2001. Evaluating the predictive accuracy of six risk assessment instruments for adult sex offenders. *Criminal Justice and Behavior* 28(4): 490-521.

Bardsley, M. 2006. *Charles Manson.* Court TV Crime Library. http://www.crimelibrary.com/serial_killers/notorious/manson/murder_1.html.

———. 2006. *David Berkowitz.* Court TV Crime Library. http://www.crimelibrary.com/serial_killers/notorious/berkowitz/letter_1.html.

Barry, C.T., P.J. Frick, T.M. DeShazo, M. McCoy, M. Ellis, and B.R. Loney. May 2000. The importance of callous-unemotional traits for extending the concept of psychopathy to children. *Journal of Abnormal Psychology* 109(2): 335-340.

Behavior Data Systems. 1996. *Domestic Violence Inventory, DVI: An Inventory of Scientific Findings.* Phoenix, AZ: Risk and Needs Assessment, Inc.

Bell, R. 2006. *Ted Bundy.* Court TV Crime Library. http://www.crimelibrary.com/serial_killers/notorious/bundy/index_1.html.

Blair, R. 2005. Applying a cognitive neuroscience perspective to the disorder of psychopathy. *Development and Psychopathology* 17: 865-891.

Blair, R. et al. 2002. Turning a deaf ear to fear: Impaired recognition of vocal affect in psychopathic individuals. *Journal of Abnormal Psychology* 111(4): 682-686.

Bloomberg, L., and S. Braaten. 1989. The effectiveness of level IV/V/BD programs in the Minneapolis Public Schools: Phase I. Minneapolis Public Schools, Special Education Department.

Boer, D.P. et al. 1997. Sexual Violence Risk-SVR-20.

Borum, R., P. Bartel, and A. Forth. 2000. Structured Assessment of Violence Risk in Youth.

———. 2002. *Manual for the Structured Assessment for Violence Risk in Youth (SAVRY).* Tampa: Florida Mental Health Institute, University of South Florida.

Bowlby, J. 1944. Forty-four juvenile thieves: Their characters and home life. *International Journal of Psychoanalysis* 21: 1953.

————. 1998. *A secure base: Parent-child attachment and healthy human development.* New York: Basic Books.

Braaten, S. 1998. *Behavioral objective sequence.* Champaign, IL: Research Press.

Briere. 1996. Trauma Symptom Check List for Children (TSCC).

Bugliosi, V. and C. Gentry. 1974. *Helter Skelter.* New York: Norton and Co.

Burns B.J. et al. 1995. Children's mental health service use across service sectors. *Health Affairs.*

Butcher. 1992. Minnesota Multiphasic Personality Inventory — Adolescent (MMPI-A).

Caputo, A., P. Frick and S. Brodsky. 1999. Family violence and juvenile sex offending: The potential mediating role of psychopathic traits and negative attitudes toward women. *Criminal Justice and Behavior,* 26, No. 3, 338-356.

CDC Youth Violence Fact Sheet. National Center for Injury Prevention and Control. Center for Disease Control and Prevention.

Children's Defense Fund. 1994. CMHS-Mental Health, US.

Child Trends Data Bank. 2006. Teen Homicide, Suicide, and Firearm Death. http://www.childtrendsdatabank.org/indicators/70ViolentDeath.cfm.

Cleckley, H.M. 1941. *The mask of sanity: An attempt to reinterpret the so-called psychopathic personality.* St. Louis: The C.V. Mosby Company.

Cline, F. 1979. *Understanding and Treating Difficult Children.* Evergreen, Colo.: Evergreen Consultants in Human Behavior.

Cocozza, S. April 2000. *Journal of Juvenile Justice and Delinquency Prevention 7* [1]: 3-13.

Commission on Behavioral and Social Sciences and Education. 1993. *Understanding child abuse and neglect.* Washington, DC: National Academy Press.

Conners. 1997. *Conners' Rating Scale — Revised (CRS—R).*

Department of Justice. 2002. Crime Clock. http://www2.fbi.gov/ucr/cius_02/html/web/offreported/crimeclock.html.

Crespi, T.D., and S.A. Rigazio-DiGilio.1996. Adolescent homicide and family pathology: Implications for research and treatment with adolescents. *Adolescence.*

Dozier, M., K.C. Stovall, and K.E. Albus, J. Cassidy and P.R. Shaver eds. 1999. Attachment and psychopathology in adulthood. *Handbook of attachment: Theory, research, and clinical applications.* New York: Guilford Press 497-519.

DuPaul, G.J, and T.L. Eckert. 1994. The effects of social skills curricula: Now you see them, now you don't. *School Psychol. Quarterly.*

Epperson, D.L., J.D. Kaul, and Hasselton. 1998. *Minnesota Sex Offender Screening Tool-Revised (MnSost-R).*

Epperson, D.L., J.D. Kaul, and S.J. Huot. 1995. *Minnesota Sex Offender Screening Tool (MnSost).*

Epperson, D.L., and C.A. Ralston. 2005. Development and scoring of the Juvenile Sexual Offense Recidivism Risk Assessment Tool - II (JSORRAT-II). Invited workshop at the Wisconsin Association for the Treatment of Sexual Abusers. Conference, Minneapolis, Minn.

Epstein, M.H. and J.M. Sharma. 1998. Behavioral and emotional rating scale: A strength-based approach to assessment. *Examiner's manual.* Austin, Tex.: PRO-ED.

Epstein, A.S. 1999. Pathways to quality in Head Start, public school, and private non-profit early childhood programs. *Journal of Research in Childhood Education.*

Fago, D.P. 1999. Comorbidity of attention-deficit/hyperactivity disorder in sexually aggressive children and adolescents. In B.K. Schwartz (Ed.), *The sex offender: Theoretical advances, treating special populations, and legal developments* (Vol. III, pp. 16-01 - 16-07). Kingston, NJ: Civic Research Institute.

Family Violence Prevention Fund. Date not listed. *Race, Income and violence: What we know and what we have to learn.* San Francisco: Family Violence Prevention Fund. http://www.endabuse.org/programs/children/files/prevention/RaceIncomeViolence.pdf#search=%22young%20caucasian%20male%020murder%20rate%22.

Flores, A.W., L.F. Travis, and E.J. Latessa. 2004. *Case classification for juvenile corrections: An assessment of the Youth Level of Service/Case Management Inventory (YLS/CMI).* Washington, DC: US Department of Justice Document 204006.

Forth, A., D. Kossen and R. Hare. 2003. *Psychopathy checklist — youth version.* Toronto: Multi-Health Systems, Inc.

Gacono, C.B. and J.R. Meloy. 1994. *The Rorschach Assessment of Aggressive and Psychopathic Personalities.* Hillsdale, New Jersey: Lawrence Erlbaum Associates, Publishers.

Gardner, F. et al. 2006. Understanding the violent offender: Early aversive history and trait anger. Conference Poster Presentation. New Orleans: APA.

Gaudiosi, J. 2004. Child Maltreatment 2004. Washington, DC: US Department of Health and Human Services. http://www.acf.dhhs. gov/programs/cb/stats_research/index.htm#can.

Gendreau, P. 1996. The principles of effective intervention with offenders. In A. Harland (Ed.), *Choosing Correctional Options That Work*. Thousand Oaks, Calif.: Sage Publications.

Glick, B. and A.P. Goldstein. 1987. Aggression Replacement Training. *Journal of Counseling and Development*.

Grisso, T. et al. 2001. Massachusetts Youth Screening Instrument for mental health needs of juvenile justice youths. *Journal of the American Academy of Child and Adolescent Psychiatry*.

Grossman, J.B., and E.M. Garry. 1997. *Mentoring: A proven delinquency prevention strategy*. Washington, DC: U.S. Department of Justice, Office of Juvenile Justice and Delinquency Prevention.

Grubin, D. 1998. *Thornton's Structured Anchored Clinical Judgment Scale (SAC-J)*.

Gunn, T. et al. 2006. Exploring ADHD and externalizing behavior in children with Sensory deficits. Conference Poster Presentation. New Orleans: APA.

Hanson, R.K. 1997. *The Rapid Risk Assessment for Sexual Offense Recidivism*. Ottawa: The Department of the Solicitor General of Canada.

———. 2000. *The effectiveness of treatment for sexual offenders: Report of the Association for the Treatment of Sexual Abusers Collaborative Data Research Committee.* Presentation at the Association for the Treatment of Sexual Abusers 19th Annual Research and Treatment Conference, San Diego, Calif.

Hanson, R.K., and M.T. Bussiere. (1998). Predicting relapse: A meta-analysis of sexual offender recidivism studies. *Journal of Consulting and Clinical Psychology, 66,* 348-362.

Hanson, R.K. and A. Harris. 2000. *The Sex Offender Need Assessment Rating (SONAR): A Method for Measuring Change in Risk Levels 2000-1.* Ontario, Canada: Department of the Solicitor General of Canada.

Hanson, R. K. and D. Thornton. 1999. *Static-99: Improving actuarial risk assessments for sex offenders.* User Report 99-02. Ottawa: Department of the Solicitor General of Canada.

Hare, R. 1990, 1991. *The Hare PCL-R, Rating Booklet.* Toronto: Multi-Health Systems, Inc.

———. 1993. *Without conscience: The disturbing world of psychopaths among us.* New York: Simon and Schuster, Inc.

———. 1995. Psychopaths: New trends in research. *Harvard Mental Health Letter, 12,* 4-5.

Hare, R.D. and C.S. Neumann. 2005. Structural models of psychopathy. *Current Psychiatry Reports* 7: 57-64.

Harris, G.T. et al. 2001. Criminal violence: The roles of psychopathy, neurodevelopmental insults, and antisocial parenting. *Criminal Justice and Behavior* 28: 4, 402-426.

Harknett, K. et al. 2005. Are public expenditures associated with better child outcomes in the U.S.? A comparison across 50 states. *Analyses of Social Issues and Public Policy*, 5 (1), 103.

Hartwell, S. 2004. *Prison, hospital, or community: Community reentry and mentally ill offenders*. Research in Community Mental Health, 12, 199-220.

Hemphill, J.F., R. Hare and S. Wong. 1998. Psychopathy and recidivism: A review. Legal and Criminological Psychology, 3, 139-170.

Hirschi, T. 1969. *Causes of delinquency*. Berkeley: University of California Press.

Hodges, K. 1995. *CAFAS: Self-training manual*. Ann Arbor: Functional Assessment Systems.

———. 1990, 1994, 2003. *Child and Adolescent Functional Assessment Scale*. Ypsilanti, Mich. Eastern Michigan University.

———. 2004. *Handbook for the Juvenile Inventory for Functioning*. Ypsilanti, Mich. Eastern Michigan University.

Hogue and Andrews. 1996. The Youth Level of Service/Case Management Inventory (YLS/CMI).

Howell, J.C., ed. May 1995. Guide for Implementing the Comprehensive Strategy for Serious, Violent, and Chronic Juvenile Offenders. Washington, D.C.: Office of Juvenile Justice and Delinquency Prevention, U.S. Department of Justice.

Howell, J.C. August 1998. *Youth gangs: An overview.* Juvenile Justice Bulletin. Washington, DC: OJJDP

Hughes, D. 1998. *Building the bonds of attachment.* Northvale, N.J.: Jason Aronson, Inc.

———. 2003. *Facilitating developmental attachment: The road to emotional recovery and behavioral change in foster and adopted children.* New Jersey: Jason Aronson, Inc.

James, B. 1994. *Handbook for Treatment of Attachment-Trauma Problems in Children.* New York: The Free Press.

Jernberg, A.M. and P.B. Booth. 1999. *Theraplay: Helping parents and children build better relationships through attachment based play.* San Francisco: Josey-Bass, Inc.

Jesness, C.F. 1988. *The Jesness Inventory Classification System.* Criminal Justice & Behavior 15 (1): 78-91.

Johnson, S.C. 1998. *Forensic evaluation: Kaczynski, Theodore.* Ninth Circuit Court of Appeals, San Francisco, Calif.

Kellert, S.R. 1997. *Kinship to mastery: Biophilia in human evolution and development.* Washington, DC: Island Press.

Kelley, B. et al. June 1997. *Epidemiology of serious violence.* Washington, DC, OJJDP: Juvenile Justice Bulletin.

Kids Count Maryland. 2006. *Advocates for Children and Youth.* Baltimore, Md.

Kohlberg, L. and E. Turiel. 1971. *Moral development and moral education.*

Kropp, P.R. et al. 1999. *Spousal Assault Risk Assessment Guide.* Toronto: Multi-Health Systems, Inc.

Kubler-Ross, E. and D. Kessler. 2005. *On grief and grieving: Finding the meaning of grief through the five stages of loss.* New York: Scribner.

Laakso, M.P. et al. 2001. *Psychopathy and the posterior hippocampus.* Elsevier Science B.V. doi:10.1016/S0166-4328(00)003247.

Leon, S.C., J.S. Lyons, N.D. Uziel-Miller and P. Tracy. 1999. Psychiatric hospital utilization of children and adolescents in state custody. *Journal of the American Academy of Child and Adolescent Psychiatry* 38: 305-310.

Levine, P. 1997. *Waking the tiger: Healing trauma.* Berkeley: North Atlantic Books.

Levy, T.M. and M. Orlans. 1998. *Attachment, trauma, and healing.* Washington, DC: Child Welfare League of America Press.

———. March/April 1999. Kids who kill: Attachment disorder, antisocial personality, and violence. *The Forensic Examiner.*

Lewin K. 1943. Defining the "Field at a Given Time." *Psychological Review.* 50: 292-310. Republished in *Resolving Social Conflicts & Field Theory in Social Science,* Washington, D.C.: American Psychological Association, 1997.

Lewis, D.O. 1998. *Guilty by reason of insanity.* New York: Fawcett Books.

Linehan, M. 1993. *Cognitive-behavioral treatment of borderline personality disorder.* New York: Guilford Press.

Lyons, J.S. 1999. *The CANS (Child and Adolescent Needs and Strengths) manual.* Ill: Buddin Praed Foundation.

Madanes, C. 1995. *The violence of men.* San Francisco: Jossey-Bass.

Marshall L.A. and D.J. Cooke. 1999. The childhood experiences of psychopaths: a retrospective study of familial and societal factors. *Journal of Personal Disorders* 13(3): 211-25.

Marvin, R.S. and P.A. Britner; J. Cassidy and P.R. Shaver, eds. 1999. Normative development: The ontogeny of attachment. *Handbook of attachment: Theory, research, and clinical applications.* New York: Guilford Press 44-67.

Massachusetts Assessment and the Massachusetts Youth Screening Instrument, Version 2.

Meloy, J.R. 2002. *Violent Attachments.* Northvale, N.J.: Jason Aronson, Inc.

Millon. 1993-2006. Millon Adolescent Clinical Inventory.

———. Millon Pre-Adolescent Clinical Inventory (M-PACI) 2005.

Mirich, D. (date unknown). Sexual Homicide. Internet Document. http://dcj.state.co.us/odvsom/Sex_Offender/SO_Pdfs/SEXUAL%20HO MICIDE,%20student%20handout.pdf#search=%22Characteristics%20of% 2036%20sexually%20motivated%20killers%20FBI%22.

Monahan, J. et al. 2001. *Rethinking risk assessment: The MacArthur study of mental disorder and violence.* New York: Oxford University Press.

Moreno, Z., L.D. Blomkvist, and T. Rutzel. 2000. *Psychodrama, surplus reality, and the art of healing.* Routledge.

Murray, B. 1999. Boys to Men: Emotional Miseducation. *Monitor on Psychology.* The American Psychological Association.

National Task Force on Juvenile Sexual Offending. 1993. The revised report on juvenile sexual offending of the national adolescent perpetration network. *Juvenile & Family Court Journal* 44: 1-120.

Newton, M. 2000. *The encyclopedia of serial killers.* New York: Checkmark Books.

Nussbaum, D. 2003. Unpublished manuscript. Dept. of Psychiatry, University of Toronto. Dept. of Psychology, York University.

———. 2006. *Recommending Probation and Parole*. In I.B. Weiner & A.K. Hess (Eds.) The Handbook of Forensic Psychology (pp. 461). Hoboken, N.J.: Wiley.

O'Connor, T.G. and C.H. Zeanah. 2003. Introduction to the special issue: Current perspectives on assessment and treatment of attachment disorders. *Attachment and Human Development* 5: 221-222.

O'Hanlon, W. 1998. *Even from a broken web: Brief, respectful solution-oriented therapy for sexual abuse and trauma*. New York: John Wiley & Sons.

Olds, D.L. et al. 2004. *Effects of home visits by paraprofessionals and by nurses: Age 4 follow-up results of a randomized trial pediatrics* 114(6): 1560–1568.

Olds, D., P. Hill and E. Rumsey. November 1998. *Prenatal and early childhood nurse home visitation*. Washington, DC: OJJDP Juvenile Justice Bulletin.

Ottley, T. 2006. *Ted Kaczynski, the Unabomber*. Court TV Crime Library. http://www.crimelibrary.com/terrorists_spies/terrorists/kaczynski/1.html.

Otto, R.K. et al. 1992. Prevalence of mental disorders among youth in the juvenile justice system. *Responding to the Mental Health Needs of Youth in the Juvenile Justice System*. Seattle, Wash.: The National Coalition for the Mentally Ill in the Criminal Justice System.

Pennison, C. and S. Welchans. 2000. *Intimate partner violence*. Washington, DC: Bureau of Justice Statistics.

Perry, B.D.; M. Murburg, ed. 1994. Neurobiological sequelae of childhood trauma: Post traumatic stress disorders in children. *In Catecholamine Function in Post Traumatic Stress Disorder: Emerging Concepts*. Washington, DC: American Psychiatric Press 353–276.

Perry, B.D. and R. Pollard. 1997. Altered brain development following global neglect in early childhood. *Society for Neuroscience: Proceedings from Annual Meeting*. New Orleans.

Pollack, S. 1998. Differences in brain electrical activity among maltreated children. *Society for Psychophysiological Research Conference* (Paper Presentation).

Pollack, W. 1999. Boys to Men: Emotional Miseducation. *Monitor on Psychology*. The American Psychological Association.

Prentky, R. and S. Righthand. 2003. *Juvenile Sex Offender Assessment Protocol-II (JSOAP-II)* Manual. Unpublished Manuscript.

Prochaska, J.O., J.C. Norcross, and C.C. DiClemente. 1992. *Changing for Good*. New York: William Morrow.

Prothrow-Stith, D. 1993. *Deadly consequences*. New York: Harper Perennial.

Quinsey, V.L. 1998. Treatment of sex offenders. In M. Tonry (Ed.), *The handbook of crime and punishment* (pp. 403-425). New York: Oxford Ariality Press.

Quinsey, V.L. et al. 1998. *Violent Offenders: Appraising and Managing Risk*. Washington, DC: American Psychological Association.

Raine, A., P. Brennan and S.A. Mednick. 1994. Birth complications combined with early maternal rejection at age 1 year predispose violent crime at age 18 years. *Archives of General Psychiatry*.

Randolph, E. 2000. *Manual for the Randolph Attachment Disorder Questionnaire (RADQ)*. Evergreen, Colo.: Attachment Center Press.

Rice, M.E., G.T. Harris and V.L. Quinsey. 2002. The appraisal of violence risk. *Current Opinions in Psychiatry*. 15 (6): 589–593.

Rich, P. 2003. *Understanding juvenile sexual offenders: Assessment, treatment, and rehabilitation*. New York: John Wiley & Sons.

Reynolds and Kamphaus. 2004. Behavior Assessment System for Children (BASC – 2).

Rones M. and K. Hoagwood. 2000. School-Based Mental Health Services: A Research Review, Clinical Child and Family Psychology Review. 3 (4): 223-241.

Ross, D. 1998. *Looking into the Eyes of a Killer.* New York: Plenum Publishing Corporation.

Ross, E. and D. Kessler. 2005. On Grief and Grieving: Finding the meaning of grief through the five stages of loss. New York: Scribner.

Roth, A. and P. Fonagy. 1996. *What Works for Whom? A Critical Review of Psychotherapy Research.* New York: Guilford Press.

Salekin, R. 2004. *Risk Sophistication Treatment Inventory (RSTI)* (University of Alabama, 150.

Schiff, G. and C. Fegan. 2003. Community Health Centers and the Underserved: Eliminating Disparities or Increasing Despair. *Journal of Public Health Policy.*

Seifert, K. 2000. *Development of the juvenile and adult CARE.* Maryland Psychologist.

———. 2003. Childhood trauma: Its relationship to behavioral and psychiatric disorders. *The Forensic Examiner.*

———. 2003. *Child and Adolescent Risk Evaluation.* Champaign, Ill: Research Press.

———. 2004. *Risk Management Evaluation — Sex Offender.* Unpublished manuscript.

———. *Subscale.* Unpublished manuscript.

———. 2006. *Child and Adolescent Risk Evaluation - Sexual Behavior Problems.*

———. 2006. *The development of the CARE and the chronic violence, sexual behavior, attachment, and psychiatric subscales.* Unpublished manuscript.

———. 2006. *School based mental health services reduce school violence.* Internet article published by NICHSA: http://www.nichsa.org/Mental-Health-services.html.

Seifert, K., S. Phillups and S.M. Parker. 2001. Child and adolescent risk for violence (CARV): A tool to assess juvenile risk. *The Journal of Psychiatry and Law.* 29, 329-346.

Serial Killer Crime Index. 2006. *Kaczynski, Theodore John.* http://www.crimezzz.net/serialkillers/K/KACZYNSKI_theodore_john.php.

———. 2006. *Manson, Charles.* http://www.crimezzz.net/serialkillers/M/MANSON_charles_milles.php.

Shapiro, F. 1997. *EMDR.* New York: HarperCollins.

Shapiro, F. and M. Forrest. 1997. *EMDR The breakthrough therapy for overcoming anxiety, stress and trauma.* New York: Basic Books.

Snyder, H.N. and M. Sickmund. 1999. *Juvenile offenders and victims: 1999 national report* (NCJ 178257). Washington, DC: U.S. Department of Justice, Office of Justice Programs, Office of Juvenile Justice and Delinquency Prevention. Also available on the World Wide Web: http://www.ncjrs.org/aspl/ojjdp/nationalreport99/toc.aspl.

Society for Social Work Research, The. 2001. *The measurement of attachment across the life span.* Internet Document, http://www.sswr.org/papers2001/420.htm.

Solomon, J. and C. George, eds. *Attachment disorganization.* New York: Guilford Press.

Stetson School. 2000. *The Juvenile Risk Assessment Tool.* Stetson School, Inc., 455 South Street, Barre, Mass.

Suicide Prevention Action Network (SPAN). 2005. www.spanusa.org.

Thomas, N. 1997. *When love is not enough.* Glenwood Springs, CO: Families by Design.

Tolan, P. and N. Guerra. 1994. *What works in reducing adolescent violence: An empirical review of the field.* Boulder, Colo.: Center for the Study and Prevention of Violence.

Trocmé, N. and D. Wolfe. 2001. *Child Maltreatment in Canada: Selected Results from the Canadian Incidence Study of Reported Child Abuse and Neglect.* Ottawa, Ontario: Minister of Public Works and Government Services Canada.

U.S. Department of Health and Human Services. 2001. *Closing the health gap: Reducing health disparities affecting African-Americans.* Washington, DC: HHS Office of Minority Health.

U.S. Department of Health and Human Services. 2002. *What You Need To Know About Youth Violence Prevention.* Rockville, Md.: U.S. Department of Health and Human Services, Substance Abuse and Mental Health Services Administration, Center for Mental Health Services.

Van der Kolk, B., J. Silberg and F. Waters. 2003. *Complex PTSD in children.* Towson, Md.: Sidran Institute.

Vernon, A. 1993. Developmental assessment and intervention with children and adolescents. Alexandria, VA: American Counseling Association.

Way, I.F. and T.J. Balthazor. 1990. *A Manual for Structured Group Treatment with Adolescent Sex Offenders.* Notre Dame, Ind.: Jalice Publishers.

Webster, C.D. et al. 1997. *HC−20: Assessing risk for violence, Version 2.* Burnaby, British Columbia: Mental Health, Law, and Policy Institute, Simon Frasier University.

Welch, M. 1989. *Holding Time.* New York: Simon & Schuster Trade Paperbacks.

West, A. 2003. *At the margins: Street children in Asia and the Pacific.* Asia Development Bank.

Wikipedia. 2006. *Charles Manson.* http://en.wikipedia.org/wiki/ Charles_Manson.

———. 2006. *Ted Bundy.* http://en.wikipedia.org/wiki/Ted_Bundy.

Wong, S. and A. Gordon. 1996. *Violence Risk Scale Experimental Version 1.* Department of Psychiatric Research, Regional Psychiatric Centre, Saskatchewan, Canada: Solicitor General of Canada.

Worling J.R. and T. Curwen. 2001. *Estimate of Risk Adolescent Sexual Offence Recidivism (ERASOR).* Version 2.0. Toronto, ON. SAFE-T Program. Thistletown Regional Centre.

Zaehringer, B. 1998. *Juvenile Boot Camps: Cost and effectiveness vs. residential facilities.* Koch Crime Institute White Paper Report. www.kci.org.

Ziegler, D. Fall 1998. Understanding and treating attachment problems in children. *Paradigm Magazine.* Huntsville, Ala.: Three Springs, Inc.

Zigler, E., C. Taussig and K. Black. 1992. Early childhood intervention: A promising preventative for juvenile delinquency. *American Psychologist.*

Kathryn Seifert, Ph.D. is a psychotherapist, author, speaker, and researcher who specializes in family violence and trauma, and has over 30 years of experience in mental health, addictions, and criminal justice work. She is Founder and CEO of Eastern Shore Psychological Services (www.ESPSMD.com), a private practice that focuses on serving children, adolescents, and at-risk youth and their families.

Dr. Seifert's articles on violence, trauma, and risk have appeared in *The Journal of Psychiatry and Law*, *Paradigm Magazine*, *Reaching Today's Youth*, *Forensic Focus*, *Self-Help and Psychology Magazine*, *The Maryland Psychologist*, and the *Forensic Examiner*. She is the author of *CARE (Child and Adolescent Risk for Evaluation: A Measure of the Risk for Violent Behavior)*, a manual and assessment tool kit that allows mental health professionals to understand the risk of potential violence in youths. The kit is widely used and trusted as a premier risk assessment test in the industry. Besides CARE, Dr. Seifert has authored and published a training DVD on disrupted attachment patterns and two guided imagery CD and journal sets.

Dr. Seifert has spoken about CARE and other related topics at conferences and seminars around the world, including the Maryland Psychological Association Presentation, the School Health Interdisciplinary Program, the 2005 Distinguished Lecture Series, the 10th Annual Conference on Advancing School-Based Mental Health, and the Canadian Psychological Association. Earlier this year, she presented a poster at the International Association of Forensic Mental Health Services in Amsterdam.

Dr. Seifert is a fellow in the Maryland Psychological Association and chair of MPA's Board of Legislative Affairs. She is a member of the International Association of Forensic Mental Health Services, the American Psychological Association, the Association for the Treatment of Sexual Abusers, the Maryland Mental Health Association, and The American College of Forensic Examiners International.

For more information about Dr. Seifert, please visit her website at *www.DrKathySeifert.com.*

About Robert Schmidt, LCPC, NCC

Robert Schmidt received his undergraduate and graduate degrees in Community Counseling Psychology. He worked for seven years at Johns Hopkins, providing direct services for School-Based Mental Health within Baltimore City Public Schools; provided primary therapist coverage to the Johns Hopkins Psychiatric Children's Center; Baltimore Adolescent Treatment Program; Outpatient Clinic and 24-hour Baltimore Child & Adolescent Crisis Response Team. Currently, Rob works as a Behavioral Specialist for a rural school district in Maryland. He provides crisis intervention, wrote and implements the county Yellow Ribbon Suicide Prevention Program, and developed a national model (outcomes-based) School-Based Mental Health Program. He presents nationally on Suicide Prevention and School-Based Mental Health Programming.